W9-BIB-514

*Flanagan My Friend*

*Also by Pat Smythe*
THREE JAYS LEND A HAND

Flanagan

# Flanagan My Friend

### By PAT SMYTHE

*Duell, Sloan and Pearce*

New York

COPYRIGHT © 1963 BY PAT SMYTHE

All rights reserved. No part of this book in excess of five hundred words may be reproduced in any form without permission in writing from the publisher.

First edition

Library of Congress Catalogue Card Number: 64-24483

DUELL, SLOAN & PEARCE
AFFILIATE OF
MEREDITH PRESS

MANUFACTURED IN THE UNITED STATES OF AMERICA FOR MEREDITH PRESS

# CONTENTS

## To PAUL

*As a token of gratitude for fifteen years of dedicated and unsparing help with the horses, especially 'our friend', Flanagan*

# ILLUSTRATIONS

# CHAPTER I

## Early Days

MOTHERS have an important part to play in forming the character of their children and Flanagan was no exception. His mother was a bay Irish draught mare, big, plain and rather common, but a great character and an honest worker on the farm. She was typical of the basic type of mare that breeds the real Irish hunter. Sadly this wonderful foundation for breeding animals of substance and quality is gradually becoming more rare. Many young ones of this type suffered from the high prices paid by foreign butchers.

Flanagan's mother first 'kicked over the traces' after her day's work was done. It was evening time and she was grazing near a bank. She thought she heard the leprechauns and looked up, but there was no leprechaun; better by far, a young chestnut stallion was looking down on her from the bank. No one would have noticed the hair around his heels as he lightly leapt down to her side. Their love was blessed and less than a year later the mare had her own chestnut colt running by her side.

The farm where they lived was only a smallholding of grass, bog and drains, crumbling banks, broken gates and a bedstead end to block one big gap in a bank. Railways and tarmacked roads did not disturb their life. Even the old byre in the small yard was too low for the horses. This background gave the colt a happy childhood while he developed into a Wexford hunter type with good substance, standing on short legs. He benefited from the limestone land that he grazed through the warm days and nights, with the grass saturated in dew, a combination of factors that makes the Irish horse what he is.

When Flanagan was two years old his mother had another interest. This was an iron grey filly foal, more classically bred than her half-brother as she was by Lansdowne, a thoroughbred sire belonging to William Bolton, who lived at 'The Island' about two miles away. The filly's grandfather was Gainsborough and the grey colour came from The Tetrarch, sire of Gainsborough's dam. The beautiful strong filly, with a lovely neck and great big brown eyes, got all the attention, and so naturally her elder brother had to find other companionship.

The soft wind that blew over the sea from the Welsh mountains also brought with it the smell of other horses nearby to the east. Already imbued with the wanderlust, the two-year-old chestnut set off one day towards the sea. He had to cope with the country of the Island Hunt, which is said to be one of the finest tests of nerve for a fox-hunting man or horse. He must have crept up and down at least twenty banks and over the big dykes before he found the promised friends. Even the brambles and hairy hedges rambling over the banks and making the dykes very blind, did not deter him.

He had arrived in a forty-acre field, part of the four hundred acres belonging to 'The Island'. The big house was built hundreds of years ago by a previous William Bolton who also started his pack of hounds there. The small ditch that surrounds the estate is responsible for the famous name of the Hunt.

The young horse was espied by sixteen thoroughbreds grazing a bog, from where they came galloping down like a cavalry charge to inspect the new arrival. He met with general approval and so became a regular visitor to these parts for the next couple of years.

A change came into his life one May morning. The squire, William Bolton, happened to visit the thoroughbreds in the field in the company of a stranger. At that time the squire was about seventy-three and a very gentle man. When he stood on the leg that had not been broken so many times as the other one, he measured about 5′ 2″ at full height. His one and only interest throughout his life was the making and breaking of young horses. This cost him four broken legs, both arms broken, one shoulder, his neck and his back. Most of these mishaps had been gathered from falls in the dykes and over the banks while out with the Island hounds.

The chestnut colt happened to be on one of his frequent visits, when the thoroughbreds were being inspected. The middle-aged, ginger-haired man with the squire was a cousin. Although this companion had come to see the thoroughbreds he asked about the rather solid and more common chestnut in their midst.

'Oh,' says William, 'that's a queer sort of a horse—he comes and he goes, you see, sometimes he's here and sometimes not.' At that moment the companion gave a sudden yell and rushed forward waving his handkerchief. In spite of the superior blood lines of the other horses, it was the common chestnut that was quickest off the mark and away. That decided his destiny. Later a rope was put around his neck for the first time and he was led to the house. After a lot of talking, a fiver was mutually split and the cousins clasped hands over a sum of £42 10s.

There were no thoughts then that a silver cup would come back in 1962 to the lowly little white-washed thatched cottage. This was to the farm, near 'The Island' in County Wexford, for the breeder of the winner of the All-England Jumping Derby at Hickstead, when Flanagan defeated Dundrum, a great-hearted little Irishman and the only other horse that had got through to the jump-off.

The journey to Northumberland that the young horse had to go through must have come as a surprise to him. Not only had he been accustomed to making his own decisions and doing what he liked, but also he had never seen or heard the wonders and the noise of the modern world.

First there was a motor horsebox that arrived to take him to Dublin. No doubt the driver who usually travelled high-class race horses was a little dubious about the quality of his cargo on that journey. Then a boat trip to Liverpool, which is rarely a comfortable crossing for either man or beast. The train that took him north-east from Liverpool must have been just as frightening. Tired from the journey and mentally exhausted by all the things that he had experienced and not really understood, he was relieved to find a person he knew when he finally arrived at his destination.

Brigadier Lyndon Bolton, his new owner, took him from the train, across the A1 by the War Memorial, along by the Castle Wall and down the road to his new home. The buses and lorries on that busy road worried him as little then as they do now. Perhaps he was only too pleased to be with a friend after the bewildering and lonely journey.

[4]

Brigadier Lyndon Bolton, Flanagan's first trainer, taking him across country in a three-day event

Early show jumping practice when Flanagan first came to me at Miserden

Spring 1956. During the training at Ascot for the Stockholm Olympic Games, talking with Colonel Jack Talbot-Ponsonby

Stockholm Olympic Games 1956. Flanagan jumping well over the Olympic water

Although the new chestnut had a plain face, it was full of character, from the tips of his long ears, and following the white star and stripe that runs in a crooked line down his nose, to the pendulous lower lip. His clown-like appearance earned him the name of 'Bud Flanagan', and not as an insult to the great artist of that name, the chestnut has been known as 'Flanagan' ever since.

The freedom of the Irish days was gone and 'the Brig' started to work on his green but unspoilt material. The horse could not have been in better hands for his breaking and early training. The experience of the trainer had been gained from a lifetime with horses, first graduating at the Equitation School at Weedon in 1923, and then spending many years as an Instructor of Riding in the Army. He had participated in many branches of the sport of riding, having won Point-to-Point races and Show Jumping events. He played polo, a great team game, and concentrated on schooling young horses, jumpers and polo ponies. Hunting played an important part too and he was Master of 'The Woolwich Drag' for four seasons. For ten years before the war and ever since he has helped the Pony Club to rise to its present high standard of young riders. After the war he was selected as a member of the British Team for the Three-Day Event at the Olympic Games in 1948, the first post-war Games that were held in London.

Flanagan could not have fallen into better hands. Naturally, as his rider was an all-rounder, he trained his horses to have the same versatility. So began the round of discipline with understanding that builds confidence and efficiency in the making of the young horse. Flanagan was subjected to a surcingle around his stomach, sometimes loose and at other times tight. He had to get used to mouthing bits that made him play with the mouthpiece and often slobber with the saliva caused by twiddling the little keys on the bit with his tongue. As the lessons progressed there were the bridle, the long reins, the lunging reins, the side reins, the saddle, the crupper and the lot.

The horse was never given a fright and having a natural capacity for enjoyment, he loved the rides over the open country with wide horizons and the fresh air. The sea was not far away and could be seen from some places, but it was the surrounding sights that kept most of the horse's attention. Most important were the other horses in the yard. There was always bustle and activity with cars coming and going and cats making their home in the hay rack, in the stables, the corner of the box or even the horse's back, as it suited the individual cat.

Lessons continued at this happy home and the horse was backed and began to learn to jump small places, which was no trouble to him after his youthful escapades solo over the Wexford banks. One day he had a bit of extra fun when being exercised early in the morning. He was about a quarter of a mile from home when he gave a buck and dropped his shoulder. Finding himself free, he galloped away along a green lane to the top of a high hill from where he could see miles of ocean. Tickled by the inspiring view, he galloped another mile and a half nearly to the railway station.

He was good enough to wait there until his hot and breathless rider caught up with him, after following his hoof tracks over the escape route. Flanagan realized that his escapade had been accomplished with success and did not take advantage again. He allowed his rider to mount and ride him home, although he had only been ridden once before.

[ 6 ]

The music of hounds was a thrill that Flanagan had enjoyed during his Irish winters. 'The Island' hounds were no strangers to him, but now he was broken and could go hunting himself.

The Brigadier lent Flanagan for the winter months to a friend who was short of a horse. The callow youngster was initiated with cubbing and then enjoyed some not too strenuous days hunting through the season. In the spring, he was turned out to grass in a big field with a companion on the best of keep. His holiday continued until July and during that time he grew and filled out.

Some of the weight that the good grass had put on his frame had to be removed with light work. Then the horse was ready for the summer holidays when the Brigadier's son took him over to ride with the Pony Club. They were happy in each other's company and did not work too hard at the more technical details of schooling.

At the Percy Hunt Pony Club Camp, Flanagan became a friend of all and with his personality, he was treated more like a dog than a horse. The work and the play together during that camp gave them the background for their first great day together. This was in the Pony Club Hunter Trials in the West Percy country. They won the competition with ease and so notched up Flanagan's first win.

The regular work and training had really developed him into a horse for the coming season's hunting. As he developed physically he became better at galloping and jumping. He was already such a good hunter by Christmas time that the Brigadier decided to prepare him for Mr Hindley's One-Day Event at Clitheroe, with perhaps Badminton as an ambitious goal in April.

His schooling became more and more exacting, with work

at slower paces demanding both obedience and activity. The mental concentration and physical effort required was quite tiring, but he never had too much of this dressage work each day to make him bored. Twenty minutes or half an hour, depending on how he worked that day, was found to be quite adequate. This was just part of his exercise that included galloping, jumping and hunting, to ring the changes. All the time he was getting strong and fit and enjoying his life.

# CHAPTER 2

# Combined Training

THE polishing and cleaning of the horse on the night before his long journey to Clitheroe must have given him an inkling that something special was in the wind. Long before dawn, the car was packed up and a very small, light, two-wheeled trailer hooked on behind. Into this went Flanagan rather dubiously as he had usually done his travelling on Shank's pony. They had a two-hundred-mile journey before them and set off at about 4 a.m.

Driving smoothly down the A1 about an hour later, suddenly everyone was shaken out of their early morning lethargy. A wheel appeared bowling alongside the car, and at that moment there was a crash and the car lurched to a grinding halt. The trailer wheel had come off and there was Flanagan trying to stand at a slant, looking out of the trailer door which had burst open. Meanwhile, the nearside wheel spun merrily down the highway.

The trailer had been fitted with new tyres the day before, because there was no spare tyre. No one had thought of tightening the nuts and, of course, there was no jack. Whereas Flanagan's more classy companions that he had left in Ireland might have panicked, he just stood stoically with one foot in front of the other along the angle of the floor and the trailer side. A four-legged tight-rope walker could not have remained more steady.

It was a lovely morning but there was not a soul in sight. The 'Brig' did not like to leave the horse alone in his precarious position and so he had to wait. An hour later a road-man appeared and was quickly asked if he knew anything about horses. He had never had anything to do with them, but agreed to watch Flanagan while the 'Brig' went off to look for the other wheel. The road-man sat down on his barrow and Flanagan maintained his tight-rope position with his head sticking out of his front door. Eventually, with the aid of a local garage, the trailer was put right and Flanagan was able to stand four-square again on the proper floor of the trailer. They continued on their way and in spite of the delay and near disaster, they arrived in time. Undeterred by their early morning experience, they won the event by a narrow margin and returned home, tired but triumphant.

This victory provided the incentive to have an outing at a full-scale Three-Day Event. At Badminton they would meet experienced and better-class horses, but the competition would be a great education. The crowds of people, swarming through the lovely park, crowding the tents and shopping lanes, and packed around the several arenas, were enough to startle a young horse. This might be the excuse Flanagan would put forward for his lack of brilliance in the dressage test.

The next day, inspired by the springy turf in the great park spreading away from Badminton House, Flanagan enjoyed his gallop over the steeplechase fences, many of which were regular fences used for the Beaufort Point-to-Point Races. The cross-country only seemed like a fast hunt to him, although he missed the music of hounds and the company of the rest of the field galloping along with him. He may have been interested once or twice during his cross-country gallop by seeing a horse ridden by tandem jockeys watching at several of the fences. That was because a kind rider had given me a hitch-hike in front of the saddle, so that I could watch Flanagan on the cross-country phase, by taking short cuts across the course, thanks to this obliging hunter and his owner. In spite of diversions such as this, Flanagan was tired after his hard day's work and longing for his supper.

Food and rest are a good remedy for many a complaint, and by the morning Flanagan was completely resuscitated. After his grooming he came out into the sun shining like copper. He felt so pleased with himself in the importance of parading around a packed arena that he struck out with his parade walk. As in a slow-march, he pointed his toes and then slapped down each foot, a swanky habit that he has continued to produce whenever he thinks that the occasion is right.

The small show jumping course gave him no problem and with a clear round, he finished eighth in the final placing. Lawrence Rook on Starlight XV won the event that April 1953. This was the year in which the European Championships were first held in this country and our team won, although in fact Lawrence and Starlight were not members of the team.

When the horses were lined up for their rosettes, one gentleman made a point of coming to Flanagan and saying, 'There is only one of these horses here that I would like to go hunting on and this is him.' The placings were forgotten and his plain looks too, as Flanagan realized that he was the centre of the picture for the moment.

His reward came as a holiday out to grass. At first he was

the boss of a thoroughbred yearling but then he was left to his own resources when the youngster was removed from the elder horse's domination. Flanagan had to turn his attention to other prey.

The house cat—a large tabby—was called 'The Marquis of Carrabas'. This was the title assumed by 'Puss in Boots' and this cat was appreciated as an equal in intelligence. Brigadier Bolton's wife was a great friend of the Marquis who kept close to her, whether she was in the house, garden or paddock. During that summer Flanagan was turned out in the steep paddock next to the house. One evening the Brigadier and his wife went to have a look at him. Carrabas accompanied them. A friend and neighbour wandered over to the group and they all started talking a few yards from the horse.

Meanwhile, Carrabas, wanting attention, had walked over to Flanagan and stood there with arched back and curled tail. Flanagan put his head down and the cat rubbed itself against his muzzle. The horse very gently picked up the cat with his teeth and then proceeded to walk stealthily forward, carrying Carrabas about six inches off the ground. The cat was suspended by the loose skin of his back, with his head, legs and tail hanging like a bunch of bananas, while he was carried at least twenty yards. The indignity of his position became unbearable and Carrabas twisted his head and spat fiercely in Flanagan's face. He had not anticipated the reaction, for Flanagan flung up his head, letting go with his teeth and throwing the cat to some height over a small tree.

Cats have a reputation for always landing on their feet. This one turned several somersaults in the air before landing on all fours with a thump about fifteen yards away. Horse and cat then stood and stared at each other transfixed.

After a minute Flanagan crept up to the cat again, but when he got too close, Carrabas decided that discretion was the better part of valour and turned up the bank. At a slow loiter he returned to the house with Flanagan following him about a yard behind. At the fence the horse was left with his apology unsaid. Carrabas must have had amazing self-confidence not to show more fear after the treatment he had been given.

The Darley Arabian, a founder of the modern thorough-bred horses, was kinder to the cat that struck up such an intimate friendship with him. It either sat on his back when he was in the stable, or nestled as closely to him as she could. On the death of the great stallion in 1753, at the age of twenty-nine, the cat refused her food, pined away and soon died.

During the summer Flanagan started work again. He was entered in a Novice competition and he won this class. A few weeks later he went to compete in the Three-Day Event at Harewood. He was much stronger and more muscled than he had been at Badminton in the spring. He galloped much faster now but although he could do his parade walk with nearly straight knees, the extended trot rather defeated him and so his dressage was never spectacular.

It was lucky that he was fit for the event, because the hilly cross-country at Harewood seemed to take much more out of a horse than the flatter land around Badminton. A fine warm autumn day accentuated the effort needed for even the 'road-and-tracks' phase up and down the hills. How-ever, the springy turf helped him to fly over the fences in the cross-country. He also put his galloping into good use over the steeplechase fences and had a very fast time. He was not too tired that night.

[ 13 ]

The next morning the horse had been entered for The Yorkshire Trial Stakes, a Grade C jumping competition in case he had not finished the course on the day before. There was the veterinary examination first and Flanagan came out bucking on the end of the lunge, and feeling his oats. As he was so full of beans, it was decided that he could do the novice competition in the morning, before doing his round over the show jumps for the final phase of the Three-Day Event in the afternoon.

He made little of the Grade C class and won it with three clear rounds. In the afternoon, over nearly the same course he had another clear which put him in fourth place for the final result of the Three-Day competition.

Ladies were now coming to the fore in Three-Day Events, a possibility that gentlemen 'military event' riders would have laughed at a few years before. In this Three-Day Event Miss Vivien Machin-Goodall won on her chestnut horse Neptune, a horse trained by Davy Jones, the most unlucky loser of the Grand National when his rein broke and he ran out at the last fence when his rider Lord Mildmay had brought him to the front, full of running. Second at Harewood came another lady rider Miss Penelope Molteno on Carmena, a bay mare that she had bought from me when I was jumping her in international show jumping events. Both these lady riders are now married. Starlight XV, the Badminton winner, and Major Rook were fifth, a place behind Flanagan.

Flanagan's consistent performance at Harewood brought him to the notice of Robert Hanson from Huddersfield. Three weeks later he drove up to Northumberland and, after seeing the horse giving a bit of a show, he liked him enough to buy the not too classy chestnut.

Flanagan had really been bought by Bob Hanson for Bill, his son. In 1953 Bill had won the Grand Prix at Rome on The Monarch, his great-hearted black horse. In the autumn of that year he and his wife Patricia had come to America with Harry Llewellyn and myself as a team. We had won the Nations Cup at Toronto, the main trophy of the tour. Bill had not been well since then and we did not know how seriously ill he was. He never really had a chance to ride the new horse.

The following September Bob asked me if I would like to ride Flanagan. I went up to Harewood and sat on him for the first time there. I was warned that he liked to have a gallop before settling down to work. Thinking that I knew better, and that a gallop would upset him before jumping, I tried to school him at a quiet canter. The result was that my liver was almost shaken through my throat. So I let him gallop, which obviously he had been waiting for, and then we settled down happily to some schooling in circles prior to entering the ring. We tied equal first in the Gamblers' Stakes—a gamble that has paid its way through our partnership.

I rode him again at Manchester a week later. The competition was held on a football ground and there was nowhere to work the horses before jumping. Flanagan has always been a bit stiff before he has had some suppling work and so this did not help him. Also at that time he would not spread over wide fences, but liked to go up and down like a jack-in-a-box. He needed work over low spreads to make him use his head and neck and I wanted to give him confidence in my riding. Through his lack of confidence over spreads, he brought down the farthest bar of a triple bar spread with his hind legs. This put us equal second, but I was well pleased with him, and realized that we needed just a little time at home to help him correct this fault.

Harringay was our next big show and would have been Flanagan's first C.H.I. Tragically, a week before the show, Bill died. Flanagan stayed at Miserden and left Prince Hal and Tosca to work with me in London at the 1954 Horse of the Year Show. They did me well that year, winning a major event each apart from Prince Hal's winning the Victor Ludorum Championship (worth £20 in those days) and the B.S.J.A. Spurs for Tosca.

I started work with Flanagan early in the New Year of 1955 as I wanted to take him with Prince Hal to Marseilles and Algiers at the beginning of April. It was a fairly ambitious programme for a horse that had never jumped indoors or at a big international show. There I would be jumping against Olympic and world champions like Pierre Jonquères d'Oriola, Paco Goyoaga and Hans Winkler.

# CHAPTER 3

# A Taste of the Future

FLANAGAN enjoyed his work that spring and had made great progress in his style of jumping and his confidence when tackling big spread fences. It is a more difficult task to cope with spreads in a show jumping arena than it is to take on the cross-country type of spreads which are limited to four feet in height. Although the ground may be rough with awkward approaches or a drop on landing, the speed of the horse can allow him to use his spare leg and get out of trouble over this height. In show jumping over big fences more accuracy and balance have to be maintained.

Pauline, my head groom, took the two chestnuts off for the long journey across France, to the port of Marseilles. I met up with them there and Flanagan had travelled very well on his first foreign trip. Prince Hal always needed a lot of work after a long journey, so I expect that Flanagan did not have too strenuous a work-out before his first entry into the huge and impressive stadium in Marseilles.

His first international competition came on April 1st, an ominous date, and was a two-horse event. Here the rider enters the ring with both his horses. In this case I rode in on Flanagan while Paul held Prince Hal. When the bell rang I started Flanagan over a very twisty course. I remember that some fences were placed at alternate angles down the centre so that I had to zig-zag across the arena facing the green horse with a new fence on every turn. Flanagan was so surprised that he twisted and sprang high over all the strange obstacles that kept appearing in front of him. Suddenly, to his relief, he found himself beside his travelling companion Prince Hal. At that moment he was astonished to find that his jockey had left him and had landed plonk on to Hal's saddle, kicking his friend away over more fences. Flanagan was just about to tell Hal about the extraordinary obstacles he had just encountered, but Paul held him firmly to prevent him disturbing the other horse while he was jumping. Meanwhile, Hal finished his course clear, giving my pair no faults. The only other rider who was clear with his horses won the competition with a faster time than mine. This was Captain de Fombelle with two experienced French Army horses.

I was delighted with Flanagan's effort and he must have enjoyed the competition too, because he has always been an expert in the event for two horses. Three years later, he was so cunning about this competition that he literally caught me on the hop. It was in Turin and I had Carousel and Flanagan there for the show. In the two-horse event I rode Carousel first, being the least experienced of the horses. To my delight he jumped a superbly fast clear over some tricky fences. Thinking I had a fast combined clear in the bag with only seven big straightforward fences to jump on Flanagan, I leapt lightly from saddle to saddle. Paul caught hold of the thoroughbred Carousel and Flanagan, anticipating my arrival, was already away before I arrived on him or had caught the reins. I did a neat backward somersault over Flanagan's onward-bound bottom and ruefully caught him later. We finished clear with eight faults for my fall and even the unbeatable Piero d'Inzeo on his native soil chalked up four faults on that day. Piero won as there were no double clears; he won nearly every other competition too, but those were won with judgment and this one was won with luck. Flanagan, in trying to be one jump ahead of the Italians, had thrown me and our winning chance over his tail.

Back at Marseilles, two days after Flanagan's first international competition, he again showed his worth. Three other well-known show jumping friends and myself arranged to get ourselves a meal between the afternoon and evening session of the show. By the time the late performance was over and the horses sent back to the stables, most places were closed for supper. So at 6.30 p.m. we piled into a minute Fiat and made our way down to the Vieux Port of Marseilles. The busy harbour is surrounded by little restaurants and we sat ourselves down in one that specialized in the local dish of *bouillabaisse*.

The proprietor insisted that we should start with *pizza*. His heavily peppered and filling flan ensured that his customers would drink a great deal of the *vin rosé* that he provided with the meal. After this preliminary, the chef staggered in carrying a load of enormous bowls of *bouillabaisse*. We were enveloped in a steam reeking of garlic as he dished out the sea food soup full of oysters, mussels, and pieces of every sort of fish. Rounds of bread were thrown in as well to sop up the soup. The garlic was an incentive for further bottles of *vin rosé* to be brought to the table.

It was late by the time we had finished the feast with *café* and the local *eau de vie* which was taken for medicinal reasons to aid the digestion, as I was told. The Fiat groaned under our weight on the return journey. Back at the

[ 19 ]

stadium we wandered in, looking contented and well fed, only to be received by furious officials, who told us the crowd had been kept waiting for half an hour.

I was riding Flanagan in this 'knock-out' event, with the winners of each pair qualifying for the next round. The eventual winner had to jump many rounds. The first into the ring was a member of our party who had done full justice to the meal. He first walked in to look at the course, still in his leather jacket but trailing his red coat in the dust. Then, unruffled by a few slow handclaps from the crowd, he rode in and won the first round brilliantly and continued unbeaten throughout the competition. Flanagan jumped extremely well considering he had never been in this type of event before. In fact the *bouillabaisse* party of four gave the crowd a run for their money and we finished first, second and equal third, leaving the other riders hungry and without prizes.

The horses had to travel to Algiers for the next show and their overnight boat trip was quite eventful. An Algerian tried to commit suicide by throwing himself off the boat. The alarm was raised and the big boat turned back. Somehow he was fished out alive after he had been in the water for more than an hour.

All the crack riders had come to Algiers, attracted by the valuable Grand Prix. On the first evening before the show opened, there was a big reception in the huge tent that housed the horses. The Governor-General of Algeria and our Consul-General inspected the well-groomed horses in their lines, with the grooms and riders lining each side of the central passage standing at the heads of the horses in their charge. Flanagan and Hal inspected with interest their perfumed rider dressed in silk instead of breeches and

Stockholm. Flanagan clearing the big parallel bars for the second time during the Olympic Event

The line-up at Stockholm, the day after the Olympic Games, when Flanagan won the first competition of the C.H.I.O. against most of his Olympic rivals

Flanagan proudly carrying his Sicilian pennacchio between his ears, against the backcloth of Monte Pellegrino at Palermo Show

Spa 1957. Flanagan helping me to win the first European Ladies Championship

boots—clothes that meant 'work'. Each horse had his name and his country's flag over his stall and there had been a competition for the groom with the best kept horses. To the chagrin of all the men grooms, Pauline, the only girl at the show in charge of horses, won this big cup with Prince Hal and Flanagan.

The next afternoon, when the horses were tied in their lines with only a pole slung between each one, Flanagan had a big fright. He had always had a loose box at home, so he was not used to being tied up. However, he was quite happy with some food in front of him. It was warm and humid and so the tent flaps had been hitched up to let more air into the stuffy tent.

Two squadrons of spahis were camping on the race-course, as they were providing 'the attraction' for the show. One of these white robed and turbaned gentlemen decided he would take a short cut through the long tent where our horses were in their temporary stabling. Suddenly he appeared like a phantom from the night, slithering under the tent flap and emerging under Flanagan's nose. The horse from the bogs had not been warned about the ways of the East and so he leapt back. His headcollar shattered as the eleven hundred-weight force of Flanagan left the rope still tied to a buckle attached to an inch of leather. The string behind him snapped as his weight hit it, and up and down the central passage he galloped screaming 'ghosts' at the top of his whinney. Pandemonium broke out amongst all the horses, but soon Paul heard that a horse was loose in the tent. She came at the double and rescued Flanagan from his race between two lines of excited horses with their kick-ing end each side of him along the passage. I went to the Show President, M. André Mathiot, and begged for a spare headcollar. He gave me an unbreakable one in rawhide, which we use on Flanagan to this day.

All types of fences were set up for the first event in the sandy arena of the Hippodrome. The jumps were quite big for Flanagan but I could give him plenty of room in the big ring. The tight turns that are necessary in an indoor arena with its limited space are more difficult for a young horse. The balance and immediate reaction necessary for taking on big fences in a small space need much more experience than when there is a distance in which the horse can be re-balanced before each fence.

Flanagan seemed attentive and ready for action as we started our first round. He was clear to the water jump. He had never seen a water jump in show jumping but I thought that his cross-country experience would serve him well over this 'natural' obstacle. In mid-air he spotted the water and must have thought that perhaps another spahi would suddenly arise from its limpid depths. He splashed a front foot into the water and, finding no solid surface, he rolled over. In getting up he trod on my leg and foot but he was all right. Luckily lame jockeys can ride, but they cannot ride lame horses.

The next day we did not have to jump as it was Good Friday. Paul took the horses to paddle in the sea, which is very good for their legs. I went to the sea too and first made a bullring in the sand where fierce sea beetles fought each other.

I left the other riders at their game and paddled into the sea to cure my swollen foot that had received Flanagan's hoof the day before. When I could stand the cold water no longer I waded back, only to find that the others had gone—with my shoes. I learnt to sympathize deeply with horses that have cast a shoe as I struggled back to the road through prickly cacti and wire grass. My retribution came on Easter Day when Prince Hal won the Grand Prix and the set of coveted gold buttons engraved with the crest of the city of Algiers. To receive this trophy we were led into the ring by a squadron of spahis—Flan's ghosts—and followed up by another squadron.

The last day finished with a Puissance and as there was no other competition for Flanagan, I entered both horses. The final battle was between Hans Gunther Winkler on Halla, a double gold medal winner in the following year's Olympic Games at Stockholm, and Prince Hal. We won this time and Flanagan was third, surprising both himself and me. The band of the Foreign Legion played 'The Queen' to honour the win and close the show.

It was little wonder that the confidence that had grown between Flanagan and myself during this tour resulted in a noticeable début in the English shows when we returned in April. On our first appearance we won the Somerset Area International Trial at the Taunton Jumping Festival, together with the Victor Ludorum Championship on the final day. In May Flanagan won the Nottinghamshire and Lincoln-shire Area International Trial for the Foxhunter Cup at Newark. Mr Robert Hanson, his owner, was President of the Society and his wife presented the cup, which gave a happy family reunion in the ring. Hal won the Newark Championship the next day, so the two chestnut boys returned home in the horse-box, boasting of their prowess to each other.

I was invited to take a horse to the White City in May, for a gala evening at the *Daily Mirror* Cavalcade of Sport. Flanagan came along to get his first experience of a floodlit arena and the venue of our International Horse Show in July.

Amongst a galaxy of athletes running, hurdling, long jumping, high jumping, came the invited show jumpers. We gave the athletes a moment to draw breath while we leapt our horses over floodlit fences. Flanagan won the competition and a good travelling alarm clock for me with the date engraved on it. Soon after that date the clock began pestering my life almost every morning, and unrelentingly it still works today and adds insult to injury by gaining time during the night. Noel Whitcomb wrote of the evening, 'We've seen Pat Smythe on a horse called Flanagan that will soon be a bigger household name than Crazy Gang Bud.' Flan reminded me as he read this that Mr Whitcomb also said that 'it took a chestnut gelding to steal 20,000 hearts when the lights flicked on' and 'a horse that will do this country credit' and 'last night Flanagan showed his paces'. So I looked up the newspaper report, and Flan had nearly got it right. Then as I read I remembered 'the deafening speedway, the five-a-side soccer, the breathless greyhound racing—all with Raymond Glendenning at the mike—hit up the excitement to a feverish peak of night, noise and excitement.'

The five-a-side soccer must have given Flanagan some inspiration because our next appearance was on the County Ground at Swindon where the Swindon Football Club was holding an important show. Flanagan won the £100 after an exciting jump-off on slippery ground in dismal rain. We returned home wet but happy.

During the round of English shows the international selection committee had decided that Flanagan was worth trying with me at a C.H.I.O. This is a Concours Hippique

Internationale Officiel with a team competition for the Nations Cup. Each country can only hold one C.H.I.O. per year. The team was going to Paris and so Paul set off with Prince Hal and Flanagan while I jumped Tosca at the Richmond Royal Show. Tosca justified my stay by winning the Ladies Competition, but in the last open class when going clear in the jump-off she stood back too far from a fence and fell, treading on my arm as she got up. At the hospital, the stud wound was disinfected and my arm X-rayed but there was no time to see the result of the X-ray before I caught the plane for Paris.

At the same time I said good-bye to Jacquie Huxley, my secretary, who was leaving to get married. Jacquie was driving Tosca back to Miserden and then handing over to Paddy Bury in the comparative calm while I was away in Paris. There has been very little calm ever since, I seem to hear Paddy say.

Paul looked askance at me when I arrived at the Grand Palais that night with a black arm swathed in bandages. In the first competition Prince Hal realized that I was not at full strength and I could not really hold him. Luckily Flanagan did not know that anything was wrong and we won three competitions during his first official international Horse Show. It is only fair to say that Prince Hal, whom I jumped in the major competitions, won one, was in our team that came second in the Nations Cup and he was also second in the Grand Prix.

It was at the Royal Show at Nottingham where Flanagan ate through his martingale. Paul had left him tied up with his saddle on, before a competition. He, being a past master at undoing any sort of knot, worked away at his rope until he was free. Then he walked over to his manger where his bridle and martingale had been put for later and he started chewing the loop of the martingale that fixes it to the girth. By the time Paul returned just before the event was due to start, the loop had disappeared down Flanagan's throat and we had to dash around trying to borrow a running martingale. All the jumpers were already tied up with theirs, but I think eventually we bought one off a saddler's stand. Flanagan was obviously disappointed that a new piece of saddlery had been produced and I was hot and bothered. The result being that we had a remarkably unsuccessful show. We blamed the hard ground because neither Prince Hal nor Flanagan could ever stand any jarring to their legs.

Between the Royal Show at Nottingham, followed by a show at Leicester, we rested the horses at Bob Hanson's Tuxford stables. He was Master of the Grove and Rufford Hunt, and we were on the way to the Great Yorkshire Show where he wanted to see his horse in competition. We had been very busy and at Leicester Flan had won the Gamblers' Stakes and Prince Hal the Open Championship. Paul thought that they could do with a change of scenery from large fences, and so she decided to turn them out for a scamper in a lovely pasture. There was an old retired carthorse there to keep them quiet. Prince Hal went out and enjoyed a roll, a buck and a kick and then some grass. Later Hal came in and Flanagan went out. After an hour or so Paul went to fetch Flan as she did not want him to fill himself with grass before travelling the next day to jump at Harrogate. There she found the carthorse, but no Flanagan.

The field was searched and she suddenly saw his happy chestnut head emerging from a pond. On closer inspection she found that Flanagan was standing contentedly in the middle, having already rolled in the slimy mud, so turning his golden coat to a stinking chocolate. She called to him, and his lower lip dropped farther. He was very happy. She made paper bag noises which are usually infallible with children or horses for drawing immediate attention. He pricked his ears and looked even more contented as he stood riveted knee-deep in the stagnant water and mud. Paul, realizing the cleaning task ahead of her, before Flanagan's appearance in front of his owner, the President, at the Yorkshire Show the following morning, in despair rolled up her trousers and removed her shoes and socks. She waded into the muddy water and collected her slime-coated horse. He looked immaculate in the ring the next morning and won a first on each of the three days including the championship. Mud, beautiful mud, it must do something to the blood.

Four days later we started jumping at the White City and it was Flanagan's first ordeal there, but he had already proved that he was ready to tackle the big courses. He won the Imperial Cup and his good performances put him in the Nations Cup, but our team was second to Italy that year. It was Prince Hal who stole the thunder by winning the National Championship and the *Daily Mail* International Championship at White City—the friendly rivalry continued between them when Flanagan took the Ladies National Championship at Blackpool, leaving Hal standing equal second. After that Prince Hal took most of the laurels, but Flanagan had already been chosen as an Olympic possible and so was rested after Harringay Horse of the Year Show.

# CHAPTER 4

# Olympics

TO be chosen to compete for one's country in the Olympic Games is the natural goal of any amateur sportsman. Flanagan has achieved this ambition twice, at Stockholm in 1956 and at Rome in 1960. These performances have involved him in six rounds over courses hardly within the reach of his physical capabilities. His brave heart that carried him through the supreme test of guts, and his preparation for the ordeal, place him at once in the select company of the bravest and best horses from other nations.

1956 was only Flanagan's second year of international jumping; and now he was faced with the Olympic Games which require all the experience and ability that can be mustered. It was the first year that ladies were allowed to compete with the men in this Olympic Event. I dearly would have liked to partner Prince Hal in this competition; however, he had not been considered reliable enough for the Games. Occasionally, when things had gone wrong, he had refused at a fence; he was, though, the most brilliant horse that I have ever ridden in my life. If, perhaps, as happened four years later at Rome, the individual and team events had been separate, then I might have been allowed Prince Hal for the Individual, for surely he was one of the greatest individual stars of the show jumping arenas.

Flanagan, with his easy temperament and buoyant schoolboy spirit, had always had a go at every fence that came in his way. Thus he was considered a safer choice for a team event, where everyone must finish or else risk the elimination of the team.

We had trained during the early months of the year and jumped a few big courses before we went to Lucerne C.H.I.O. for a final training in international competition. I was allowed to take Hal along with me and won the Puissance with him and I also rode him in a team event that we won.

With Flanagan I won the Grand Prix Militaire, in which previously ladies were not allowed to compete. Ladies, now being allowed to jump in the Olympic Event, became eligible for a major Cup Event. Although an Italian girl was second to me, the third place was taken by Capt. de Fombelle of France. He holds the honour of being listed in the programme since then, as the Official winner of the Military Grand Prix that year! Our team won the Nations Cup there and felt that we were further prepared for the Olympics.

Flanagan had his worrying moments after arriving at Stockholm. While we were waiting for a parade, a terrific thunderstorm drenched us all and Flanagan must have caught a chill on the kidneys. This was only a few days before his big event and it was touch and go whether he would be right in time. Just after the first scare about his kidney trouble, a big riding school next to where our horses were stabled caught fire. Our horses had to be quickly removed outside until the cascade of sparks from the collapsing roof of the school had subsided. Paul, ever watchful over the horses' welfare, kept Flanagan walking around to keep him warm and then was able to return to the stables when they were considered to be safe from the fire.

A thunderstorm had made the ground very difficult by the time Flanagan had to enter the vast and crowded stadium for his and my first Olympic round. He was faced with a course made for a free jumping athlete like Prince Hal and he was sure to be hampered by his own short stride. These doubts, even if they are certainties, cannot be entertained in an Olympic event. He had the ability to try and his pluckiness got him through in spite of his lack of real ability.

He justified the selectors' choice in his trustworthy tackling of these fences. He nearly fell at fence No. 5, a double of very big rustic parallel poles with the longest allowable distance for one stride between them. He increased the number of Swedish matchsticks that this fence had occasioned. Splintered poles were once more scraped from the surrounding area by the patient Swedish arena party, while two more chaps trotted on, carrying a new lot of rustic poles from the dwindling pile outside. Flanagan continued undeterred by the activity of the soldiers and picked his nose out of the mud, gathering himself for the next problem a few seconds ahead. This fence was a 7' open water with a 5' post and rails on the far side. He finished the tremendous course with eight faults, which up to then had been one of the best scores.

Stockholm had lines of fences built for horses with a long galloping stride. Flanagan was pushed to his utmost by the last jumps in each line as it was not possible to put in an extra stride and yet he was not close enough to the last huge spread to reach the far pole. This was his undoing at the twelfth fence in the second round when he was clear as far as the treble jump. Once we had sorted that problem, the final two fences he jumped clear and helped the team to a bronze medal. I am still wondering how I could have got more impetus for that twelfth fence, and so have achieved a clear Olympic round.

It was twilight for our presentation of the medals and Flanagan proudly pointed his toes in his best parade walk. A week earlier we had paraded with all the twenty-nine competing nations, when many fresh horses had misbehaved, excited by the music of the military bands. Our nation being Stor-Britannia in Swedish came next to the Swiss team, where a friend was riding a chestnut mare that he had bought from me only a year before. They completed the course for the Three-Day Event although their team were not in the medals. This was proof, I pointed out, of the versatility of horses trained for show jumping. 'Cuckoo,' said the clock as I put this on paper!

In the arena that we had left in the twilight, Flanagan jumped two days later. It was the first international competition of the Stockholm C.H.I.O. in which the Olympic horses could compete. Not only had the ground dried up considerably but the course was of Official International standards and not of the Olympic standard. Flanagan came out to win the 'Hederspris'. He beat all his Olympic opponents of a couple of days before, except for Halla whose rider was resting. Flanagan had not been frightened by his efforts—he was merely pleased to meet another course that was within his scope this time! We won the Nations Cup there too, after a jump-off against Italy—Flanagan was clear both times. His good results added to Prince Hal's during the C.H.I.O. gave me the ladies prize. It was the last presentation of the Olympic year in that arena.

[31]

Our team, training before the Rome Olympic Games in 1960, again started with jumping at Lucerne for the first C.H.I.O. of the season. Flanagan fulfilled a great ambition of mine by winning the Grand Prix of Lucerne. Many Swiss friends were delighted by his performance too, and it was relayed on the television. The elegant clock that he won is now chiming in the drawing-room and its colour matches our bracket wall-lights.

The gentlemen riders at Lucerne were well protected from the danger of a lady stealing their thunder. My results throughout the show gave me the most points for the sash of the leading rider. But, alas, the points had been channelled into two prizes making a leading lady and a leading gentleman rider the winners. This prevented the possibility of a lady winning the more honourable premier award at a big international show just prior to the Olympics. There was much leg-pulling on this account between the riders. Some of the men said, 'Well we need protection and this is the only civilized show that gives it to us!'

The White City was our next C.H.I.O. where again Flanagan went consistently well in the big events, winning two. The Prince Hal Stakes which he appropriately won was named after his old stable companion. In the Queen's Cup with the fastest round in the jump-off, a heel on the tape of the water jump cost him the honour of the Cup. He made amends by winning the *Country Life* and Riding Cup in spite of a thunderstorm during his round. I was also riding Scorchin for the first time since I had enjoyed riding him so much prior to the 1956 Olympics. He came out with a smile on his face winning the *Daily Mail* Cup for me, causing a general surprise. These combined results made me the runner-up to David Broome in the Loriners

Cup. Equal with me was the American Team captain, Bill Steinkraus. Flanagan was also equal third for the saddle of honour. Two years later we were destined to win both these awards.

At Dublin the following week we reversed the placings with Flanagan making me the leading rider with David Broome the runner-up. Flanagan had won the first and last competition and his general consistency made me the proud wearer of the blue and white sash.

We flew the horses to Rome and Flanagan travelled as well as ever. When we arrived in the terrific hot spell that was stifling the city, I was afraid that he would suffer from the heat, as well as the dry and therefore hard ground. Luckily a thunderstorm improved the ground before the Olympic Individual competition.

That day had started for us riders in the Piazza di Siena at 6 a.m., the scheduled time for walking the course. The sun was just peeping over the umbrella pines and making a sparkle on the dewy grass. We were not let into the arena until ten past six but meantime we had studied the plan of the course, pinned to the notice-board. It was still quite cool and I was glad to have on my wind-jacket over my riding-coat. 'Vai,' said an Italian voice and we all surged into the ring on foot. The first three fences were quite straightforward and then a very large water with only a tiny hedge in front of it came as the fourth fence. Very few horses cleared this during the competition. Then an unimpressive narrow gate close after the water was followed by brown parallel bars that caught a lot of horses, as it was difficult to see the front pole. Now came the problem fence, a combination of a wall, a triple bar and then a parallel bars. The problem was the distance between the last two parts. It was too long for one stride, except for a flying machine like Sunsalve, and too short for two strides still keeping enough impulsion to get out over the wide parallel bars.

Riders gathered in anxious groups discussing how to ride this combination. I saw one of the Russians stepping out the distance for a fifth time; he hoped that he might have counted wrong the other times. We knew that he had not made a mistake, as we had already measured between the fences.

'*Nee ochen kharasho?*' I asked him, selecting three of about the ten Russian words I know.

'*Nee ochen kharasho,*' he confirmed gloomily, meaning— not very good. Forty minutes later one of his compatriots was lying unconscious on the spot where we stood, having had a bad fall which knocked him out.

Indeed we all had good cause for anxiety because this fence spoilt the competition. Many horses fell here including the German Meteor, team gold medal winner from Stockholm. Halla, the double gold medallist, was also caught by this. It was not the fault of the Italian course builder, as his original distance, which was quite reasonable, had been changed to this almost unjumpable distance by the technical delegate of the F.E.I. (International Equestrian Federation). The rest of the course was big and of Olympic proportions but fair to the horses if they were properly ridden.

The seats of the Piazza di Siena were not filled by the time the first horse was jumping. He had 29¾ faults and the next horse was eliminated. Fifth to go was Raimondo d'Inzeo on Posillipo and with astonishing ease and to the admiration of all, he jumped a classical clear round. Only the early birds who arrived before 7.30 a.m. saw this round, and it was to be the only clear of the day and the 1960 Olympic equestrian jumping events.

Sunsalve was the first of the British horses, and David Broome took him round for 16 faults. Halla had 17 faults and then The Rock and Piero d'Inzeo did the second best round for 8 faults.

It soon came round to Flanagan's turn, and I was feeling that it was a bit unkind to ask him to jump a course beyond his physical capabilities. He soon dispelled that fear, taking on the fences like a lion. Unfortunately he tried to take only one stride in the last part of the treble in spite of my firm restraint, obviously thinking, as did many other top horses, that the set distance was hardly credible without themselves or the fences falling, but lack of experience or intelligence seemed to be almost an asset with this trick distance. Flanagan had already landed almost at the foot of the third element of the treble and the big parallels. How he kept his feet while in that tangle of bars is more than I can imagine. I have a film of this round which tells its own story.

A photographer took a picture of us, with Flanagan nearly falling, and I used this photo for my 1960 Christmas card with the caption 'Look, no hands'. Luckily I dropped the reins and just kept my balance whilst allowing him full freedom of his head to get back on to his feet and free of the obstacle. He jumped the next fence clear—a wide parallel bars over water. That afternoon he was less fresh and more obedient and so we negotiated the treble without fault. It had caused as much trouble to good horses as to the bad ones and a few riders did not enjoy the effect of their falls there. Flanagan, having as nearly come to grief in the

[ 35 ]

morning as he had in his Stockholm first round, still retained his sense and courage to try his utmost in the afternoon. He almost stood on his head to get over the third part of the treble, and somehow he succeeded.

It proved his tremendous courage that he should tackle that fence without fear. Instead of being frightened by his bad mistake in the morning which must have hurt him, he had learned from it. Retaining all his boldness, he realized that he would have to obey me.

The team event at Rome did not produce an official clear round but Flanagan managed to get twice round the course without too high a score. Although our team was eliminated by the first horse Franco having three refusals, we still had to jump the two rounds. So many teams had been eliminated after the morning round that the authorities were afraid that there would not be enough jumping to entertain the capacity crowd in the afternoon. For those interested in the mechanics and training of show jumpers, it would indeed have been a wasted afternoon if they had not seen all the riders. Those from behind the Iron Curtain and distant South American countries were seldom able to compete in Europe.

The Mexicans, gold medal team and individual winners at Wembley in 1948, had no team. In the first Olympics after the war we had seen them jumping with precision and demanding complete obedience from their horses. They would need more speed in their approach now, in order to have the impetus to jump the big spreads set in this course. However, the country had not been settled enough to think of producing an Olympic Equestrian Team.

From the obedience demanded by the Mexican riders, the style of the Russians came as a great contrast. They

March 1958 in Davos with Flanagan winning the Prix de Parsenn

Flanagan needing sun-glasses at the following year's Spring Show on the snow in Davos. Pauline Sykes and Carousel are sympathetic

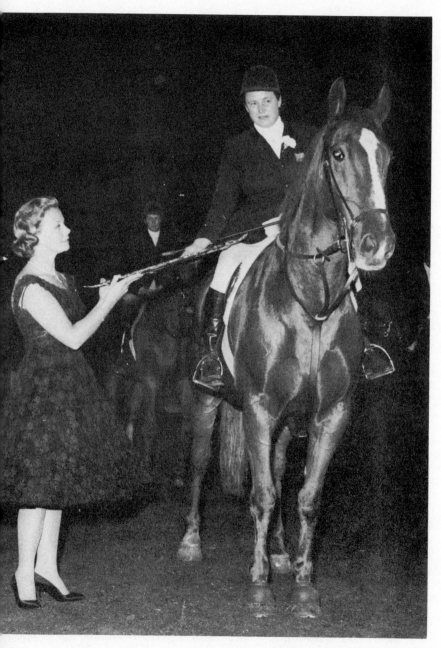

embley 1959. Flanagan winning the William Hanson Trophy, presented by Bill's
widow, Patricia

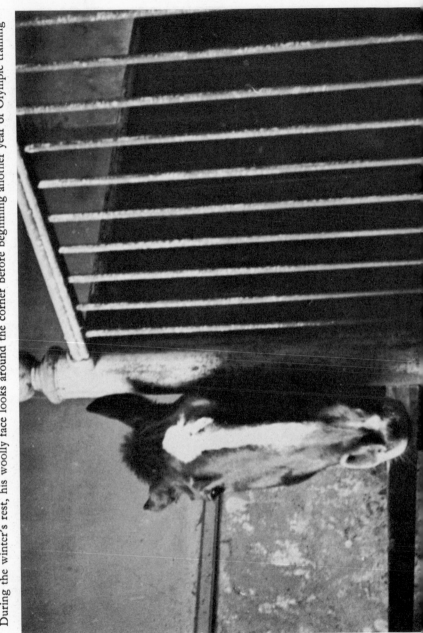

During the winter's rest, his woolly face looks around the corner before beginning another year of Olympic training

rode little active horses, which they galloped over the courses, without much placing from the rider. The riders sat well forward and the little horses needed the speed to get impulsion over the big fences. They were often unbalanced as they came to combinations of fences and even the threat of Siberia did not always sort out their double and treble trouble. Neither horses nor riders had the experience of riding over courses of this difficulty. In Europe we are always jumping against the best in international shows and therefore courses must be difficult in order to find a winner. The Russians have been improving but still they will need more international competition to produce a top team for Olympic Games. It is a necessary experience for them to come to Western Europe where they will meet and compete against the top international riders. Also they need to jump more often in competition over big courses to prepare them for Olympic difficulties.

The United States are lucky in having wealthy people to help finance their team training. They have private individuals who can buy expensive horses for the team. While the team train together the horses are allotted to suitable riders. Then the team can spend the summer months touring the European shows. They have been lucky and wise in finding Bert Nemethy as a trainer. He came from Hungary and has the knowledge and the discipline of international show jumping at his finger-tips and this he puts over to the riders in his charge. The U.S. Team has been much admired for its uniformity of style and fluent, attractive riding. Its advantage comes from riders and horses being together for so much of the year with the one talented trainer.

The gold medallists of Stockholm and Rome were the

German Team. They rely on individual riders who, when they have shown that they can win, are provided if necessary with good horses by the Federation. Their Federation is rich and consistently has bought the promising horses produced in Germany. The riders lack a uniform style and are often rough and unattractive to watch as they perform. This may be necessary treatment for the mentality of the German horse. Their results prove that they have not suffered from the severe discipline in training and competition. The horses are able to jump very great heights but seem to need complete domination by the rider, in order to carry out their job.

Italy has had its name carved in present-day international show jumping by the d'Inzeo brothers, who have been top winners since the last war. Their father was an instructor in the army and brought up the boys within the army school. So often a boy will give up riding if he is pushed into it, but these boys were two exceptions in every way. They have the natural gift of riding any type of horse, and giving it confidence for jumping. They are lucky in that the army supports them and that the horses are bought for them. Without their gift for show jumping they would gain little benefit from this support. The Italians spend vast sums of money on buying horses, but in spite of this there are few other Italian riders who can support these two brothers in a team event. Money does not buy the determination to win under any circumstances which is an inherent quality of the d'Inzeos and any top-class international show jumping winner.

Ireland is the source of many of the best horses in the world, and although the Irish have a regular army team for international jumping, since the war it is their civilians who have made the greatest mark.   There are several cases in the world where the best facilities and greatest training grounds never produce great and lasting winners.   The ones that go to the top and often remain there may have first learnt to jump over petrol tins and larch poles poached from boundary land.   With the limited scope of these beginnings a horse has to learn complete obedience over an odd selection of small fences.   The resulting confidence acquired with a rider who cannot afford the luxury of jumping complacently over a proper set of fences, has often produced a good winning combination.   A person who does nothing but ride and train all the time may be penalized in the long run.   In a moment of crisis a split-second decision is needed. Then the rider with initiative will react instantaneously. He may have to work at other jobs all day to gain his living and therefore he is mentally more alert to get the utmost from his sport.   A chap whose life is involved entirely with horses, may let theory take the place of reaction; meanwhile, the chance of winning has passed him by.

No amount of training can teach the rider to possess a fighting spirit and will to win, but training will prepare both horse and rider to be ready for a winning effort. Although a good rider on a bad horse will occasionally win, and a good horse will sometimes give a poor rider a victory, only a good combination of horse and rider will take them regularly to the top places.   This factor of a partnership will always make this sport an interesting spectacle.   Every horse is different and the rider must understand each individual to get the best results.   Once an understanding and a discipline has been established then confidence between them will develop.

Flanagan and I had become friends very quickly.   I knew

[ 39 ]

his limitations and was careful not to ask him to make extravagant jumps over the early courses that we tackled. I knew well that he found wide spreads difficult to reach, because he has a short neck and back. A long-backed horse finds it much easier to stretch itself over a fence. I jumped many small spreads on Flanagan, teaching him to stretch over them. Never did I ask him to take off too far from the fence. I tried to build his confidence in my judgement and to show him that I was not going to ask more of him than required for each fence. When the spreads got bigger I let him have more speed but kept at the same time a balanced, accurate stride, so that the impetus would help him over, without the increased pace becoming a penalty to accuracy.

At Rome such pageantry as great parades on horse-back had not been accorded to us. Marching masses of athletes opened the Games and the emphasis was naturally placed on the competitors on foot. Although the equestrians did not have the limelight as in the Equestrian Games at Stockholm, the last afternoon at Rome proved to be an experience of a lifetime.

We were already eliminated as a team and therefore out of the competition. Perhaps the ordinary spectator does not imagine how deflated one can feel, when the fire of competition has been extinguished. A rider who loves his horse would naturally feel resentful if he has to subject the horse to an unnecessary risk. I knew that the circus could provide thrills if that was what the public required. We were to perform an act, outside the actual Olympic competition but over the Olympic fences. This act involved Flanagan and I had now to demand the utmost from a horse with a brave heart, rather than athletic ability—without

hope that our effort, however gallant or good, could aid
or hinder our team in any way.

A sportsman does not go to the Olympics to become an
exhibitionist, but we were being reduced to that status,
although we could bring no honour with medals to our
country.

Few people in their right frame of mind would tackle an
Olympic event—ALL OUT—when the result did not count.
If they did, I feel that their intelligence might be suspect.
This factor applies to any branch of top international
competition.   Guy Perillat, the champion skier from France,
hurt his knee during training just before the big international
race for the Lauberhorn Cup at Wengen, Switzerland.   He
did not partake in the 'once down the course' training run
allowed to the competitors on the day before the race.   His
knee probably would not have stood the strain, although he
missed the great advantage of knowing the course and the
speed of the snow just prior to the event.   During the race
the next day he forgot the pain from his knee in the thrill of
the competition.   He was racing against the best and with a
superhuman effort of concentration and skill, he won the
race.   The will to win can override many a disadvantage.

In the stadium at Rome, the amateur riders from the dis-
qualified teams were being used for financial means to
appease the paying public.   Baron de Coubertin had not
intended the Games to be interpreted in this way.   Yet
civilians, comfortable in the financial sense and on the
Olympic committee, can easily debar a sportsman from
competing.   It is difficult for us to understand how teams
of riders compete as amateurs when they are kept uniquely
for equestrian sport, with horses bought for them, and their
lives financed and organized so that they need do nothing

but train for this sport. On the other extreme one finds the ordinary person who works himself mercilessly in order to keep a horse or two. He is told that he is a professional if he spends any time in teaching people to ride, which would not help his own riding or the training of his top horses. In doing such work, not only is he a professional, but also he is at a complete disadvantage when competing against the army officer or state-sponsored rider who does nothing else but ride horses in training for big events. The latter is an amateur who has no financial outlay or worries because horses are provided for him and his life is secure.

I do feel that there is much hypocrisy surrounding the label of 'amateur' and that the term needs to be clarified. The few sportsmen who actually compete for the love of the sport are usually the people who are most penalized by the few vague statements made to salve the conscience of committees.

These thoughts came to me later and meantime I had an immediate responsibility. Ahead was a terrific course of fences simmering in the Roman heat of the afternoon, with a hundred thousand people watching. The silence of the crowd as Flanagan and I walked down the long ramp into that arena was impressive. Someone whistled 'Cherie, je t'aime, cherie, je t'adore', which could have been embarrassing in the quietness of the crowd, but I had other things to concentrate on and the most important was Flanagan. I was the only girl in the team event and Flanagan had to jump an efficient round.

He started to get his tongue over the bit in the excitement of jumping, but his round was good for a course of this size. My heart missed a beat at the biggest double of spread fences, when his hind leg displaced a square of turf which had been previously removed for the shot-putters during their event. I thought that all was lost as his hind leg gave under him bringing him to a momentary halt. With a terrific effort he launched himself when I asked him to take off; bravely he cleared the first part and only had down the second element of the second fence. He finished clear over the other fences and no one was more proud than I of his six great Olympic performances.

# CHAPTER 5

# Conversazione

THE stables at Rome with Flanagan being led in by Paul. He looks a little tired and is blinking flies out of his eyes. The humidity is not helping him to cool off after his Olympic effort.

*Scorchin* Ciaou, chum! Jumped any good Olympic rounds lately?

*Flanagan* You idle old carthorse—sitting here in Olympic stables while we went and worked in the heat of the midday sun.

*Scorchin* Midday sun, you old flat foot, it was the dark before dawn when you woke us all, by being fed and groomed, with Paul fussing around you. She hardly laid a brush on me, but anyway my temper would not have stood much of the early morning treatment.

*Flanagan* All that and a few small fences—brother, you don't know the meaning of Olympics.

*Scorchin* Use respect when you speak to me—you forget about my having an Olympic bronze medal from Stockholm.

*Flanagan* Yes, and hit the last two straight and easy fences which lost us a silver.

*Scorchin* Now you just keep quiet. If only the climate was cooler, I'd have a quick reply for that statement, *amico mio*!

*Flanagan* As I was telling you, the course was big, as it

should be in a Grand Prix des Nations. However, the zip had gone out of the competition from my point of view, even in my early round.

*Scorchin* What zip, you lazy old blighter.

*Flanagan* That I'm not sure about, but some sort of zip. Anyway I amused myself by discovering a game of my own. I was a bit excited by the atmosphere of terrific crowds and the obvious importance of the occasion, so I started, out of bravado or nerves or something, to fiddle with my bit. I got my tongue over it and then we were off. I found that I could hardly be disciplined when I hung my tongue over the bit and I was most amused.

*Scorchin* You should have put it in your cheek where it belongs.

*Flanagan* Well, actually, I did find a bit of trouble when I had won with my tongue and then found that because I hadn't been obedient, I had to make far more effort to get over those fences.

*Scorchin* Pity it wasn't me, because I find it no trouble to get over THOSE fences.

*Flanagan* Extraordinary that you weren't considered good enough to have a go—isn't it, old pal. (*Horse laugh!*)

*Scorchin* Others before me have suffered my fate too.

*Flanagan* Don't be bitter, just because I've done all the work. Here you are in jolly Rome, and I've been told that when in Rome, it is not necessary to do as the Romans. So sleep well, my friend.

Scorchin was already in the land of Olympic fences, where every obstacle was made for the joy of jumping and within his easy scope. A happy smile played around his whiskers.

## Flanagan's Friends

FLANAGAN has made a great difference to the character of Scorchin since they have travelled the shows together. Somehow he has developed Scorchin's sense of humour, which on occasions has caused his own leg to be pulled rather harder than he expected. Scorchin had to put up with a lot. At first it was degrading for him when so often Flanagan won the big battles of the ring. At night Flanagan would boast of his prowess, then while Scorchin looked away, sadly regretting the moment when he had lost the competition by hitting the last fence, Flanagan would remove his friend's headcollar. In the morning Scorchin would have all the blame for getting free.

When Scorchin started to get his fair share of the laurels, his sense of humour blossomed and he often turned the tide on Flanagan. During last winter while they were turned out together, I have watched them from my window. After they finished their boxing match, done in play and goodwill, Flanagan would turn away for a breather and a bite of grass. Then Scorchin would edge up behind him and catch hold of Flan's dock—the tail bone. In spite of Flan's indignation and surprise, he would not let go. Flanagan's angry looks would turn to action, bucking and humping his back. He would then trot off, but Scorchin still followed benignly with the tail in his mouth.

There was an international show at St Gallen in Switzerland where I took Scorchin, Flanagan, Telebrae, and Bayridge. They were stabled in stalls and one night Flanagan removed Scorchin's headcollar. In the morning Paul found Scorchin happily helping himself to the store of hay, while Flanagan dribbled with frustration, tied to his empty manger, listening to the sounds of munching.

Flanagan dribbles frequently at the thought of food. There was a time once at home when he spent a lot of time and dribble on one of our stable cats. We had been given a long-haired black kitten by our corn merchant. She became a good mouser and seemed to be quite content with her stable life. Then one night, destiny, in the shape of Flanagan, changed her life.

Somehow she had been shut into Flanagan's box. He took advantage of the situation as he had nothing better to play with and so he must have licked her all night. The morning revealed a miserable cat with her long coat screwed into tight wet curls, making her look skinny and unattractive. This permanent wave did not last long, but our ginger Manx cat, Linx, must have been taken in briefly by her curly looks. He wooed her to become a house cat and live in comfort with him. The opportunity of a lifetime must be taken during the lifetime of the opportunity. Brigitte took her chance, and has lived in splendour ever since. She is often found lying in an armchair enfolded in the paws of Linx. She finds more fulfilment from this love than from the salivary tongue of Flanagan.

Flanagan may have told Scorchin about his night's licking of Brigitte. I took Scorchin and Bayridge to jump at Davos, where they were in stalls together. The cow stalls had very low partitions and Scorchin had to be tied very close to the side where Bayridge stood. He spent the first night licking the fine woolly winter coat of Bayridge, to the other's annoyance. In the morning Paul had to brush out the tight curls all down that side of his neck.

Salt is a great attraction and often a necessity for some horses. Flanagan eats rock salt in lumps and will happily chew whole pieces. This love for salt may be a reason why he will lick your hand or hair for as long as you let him dribble over you. The experts would say that he has a salt deficiency in his diet, but as he eats everything within reach, perhaps science has not touched on his problem yet. Unfortunately for him, he puts on weight as he breathes and so his food has to be strictly rationed. He is always hungry and it is pathetic to hear him shouting for food. If he was given all he asked for he would get too heavy for flight over the fences.

Flanagan does have one aversion—trams. He has no fear of anything but if he hears a tram in the distance, his eyes light up. This is the excuse to play up and pretend to be wildly frightened. At Lucerne C.H.I.O. there is always a long ride from the stables, right through the town to the show ground. Along the route trams often clatter by. The dangers to which Flanagan subjects himself, while acting the goat on the tarmac when a tram is in the vicinity, are a bad insurance risk. Pauline dreads any journey within earshot of a tram.

He is even worse if the show goes well and he wins a big prize. It is only after winning an important competition that he goes berserk when I get off him. He is no respecter of persons while excited thus, so will swing round knocking over anyone in the vicinity. This irresponsible behaviour is only produced on really big occasions. On one of these occasions he had previously grabbed the carnation off my coat and devoured it with the wire and trimmings. He then jumped the course with even greater vigour than usual and suffered no ill-effects.

Animals play a large part in the lives of these horses. Another stable kitten, who also came from a wild litter born in the storage barns of the corn merchant, was named Wigs. He became civilized fairly quickly but just when he began to trust his human friends, Paul had to take the horses to Ascot for the four days jumping at the beginning of the season. Wigs came too, in the box. At Miserden Post Office, a letter had to be posted. A routine check was made to see that the horses were comfortably settled for their journey. The horses were happy but Wigs was not there. A quick plan of action was formed, to make certain that all the countryside was searched for the cat. Someone wandering along the road said, 'What's all the fuss?' 'The cat has disappeared,' was the worried answer. 'Well, you've got a black one sitting under the box,' came the unruffled comment. It was Wigs.

The country kitten was introduced to Ascot and the maze of horseboxes, housing more people than our village at home. He stood the lack of calm for two nights, but was nowhere to be found on the third day. We sadly thought of the perils of the London–Ascot road but the country-bred cat had not risked the danger of modern civilization. He merely asked to be let back into the horsebox and please could he have some milk—some twenty-four hours later. He is with us still.

Fina La Ina, the Lucas terrier, also feels that we need her support at the shows. Often she does come in the box, and she loves a good long journey, when she can press her nose against the windscreen, leaving breath marks that are far from transparent, while she looks out for all points of interest. On one occasion, the weather was very wet and the dogs were sensibly left at home in comfort. Miserden Post Office was kind enough to ring Paddy to say that the horsebox had gone by with a small sandy terrier galloping after it. Paddy got into the car and drove up the road. A mile or so farther, there she found Fina still galloping.

Fina was grateful when Paddy opened the car door for her to jump in. Perhaps she realized the frustration of fighting against reality, when the box was already ten miles away, with more than 150 miles to go. Still, when Fina has an idea, she likes to carry it out. If someone comes to save her from a frustrating failure, she is never bitter but only very pleased.

# CHAPTER 6

# All at Sea

AFTER the Olympic Games at Stockholm and its exertion I did not want Flanagan to be tired and stale at the White City. When Mr Hanson had seen him win the Great Yorkshire Championship from Prince Hal, the horses needed a short rest. I too decided to change my occupation.

My cousin John had mentioned that he was going to sail his boat to Dieppe. I suggested that he should stay with a family whom I knew lived near the little harbour of Le Tréport. My French friend Brigitte and I had already explored many out-of-the-way places together, but I had never been to her home. Luckily I overheard John saying that although he had a navigator called Martin, he needed a third person as crew. I jumped at the chance and promised to get to Cowes as soon as I had finished jumping at Harrogate. The horses were in great form, which meant I had to stay until the last jump-off on the last night. I was supposed to meet the others in London, first thing in the morning, hence my hurry down the Great North Road to go south directly the Championship jumping had been decided. We had to get to Cowes by the right tide the next day. I did not know the times of the tides, in fact I knew very little about boats or sailing.

I drove away through the dusk, passing the heavy vehicles ploughing their way through to their destinations, surrounded by clouds of smoky diesel fumes as their engines hammered out the vibrating power to chug up steep hills and steady them down the other side.

Having been a lorry driver myself, it always pleased me to see the politeness and good driving of the heavy vehicles —the more cumbersome the lorry, the better manners of the driver were nearly always noticeable. When driving the horses, it is most important not to brake quickly, or they lose their balance. The most trouble would be caused by the charabanc drivers who cut in on blind corners and nearly pushed one off the road. At night with the lorry, the other drivers would always have a chat by flashing their lights as I passed, but now in a car there was no time for this friendly way of conversation.

With a brief stop for sleep, I arrived in London to find that John and Martin had already left. It was Friday, the 13th, but I hopefully got the next train to Southampton.

At the port, it was raining, although by the time the ferry reached Cowes, the drizzle had stopped, leaving a cold misty evening shrouding the deserted little boats anchored in the harbour.

I made my way to Uffa Fox's house to wait for John. Uffa was away in France, but I changed into a sweater and trousers, and glanced at one or two sailing books, confirming my fears of how little I knew about the sport. Looking out of the window I saw a launch coming to pick me up, with John and Martin dressed in oilskins crouching in the bow. Leaving the shelter of the house, I shivered as the wind whipped through my short duffle-coat. The sea spray had soaked me by the time I had climbed into the launch, and we were speeding towards *Ayesha*. She was moored quite far out and after the launch had abandoned

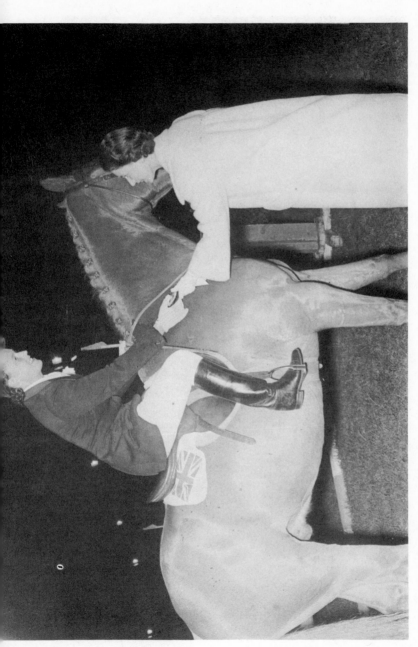

Training for the 1960 Olympic Games. H.M. the Queen presenting us with a rosette after a display round at the Royal Windsor Horse Show

Lucerne C.H.I.O. 1960. Winning the Grand Prix of Lucerne

Lucerne C.H.I.O. 1960

White City Royal International Horse Show 1960. A heel on the water tape costs him the Queen's Cup

'Look, no hands!'

The Individual Event in the Piazza de Siena, Rome Olympics 1960. After nearly falling at the treble, Flanagan bravely stretches over a wide double of parallel bars

Individual Olympic Event. Having cleared the difficult treble on his second round in the afternoon, he confidently jumps the following fence

Jumping in the packed Olympic Stadium for the Team Event at Rome

us aboard, we set about getting the boat ready for sailing and having a quick meal before leaving with the tide.

Eventually we cast our moorings at about 9 p.m. and set our course to the East, sailing down the channel between the mainland and the Isle of Wight.

The difficulty of keeping a set course in a strong wind was accentuated by the nearly non-existent battery light of the compass. We had an anxious moment when we thought some lights marked the first of the forts, and yet from our calculated position we had not yet arrived there! On approaching nearer, the lights showed a liner, large enough to house a garrison, anchored in the channel, so we sailed on finding, to the credit of our navigator, the correct buoys exactly where they should have been. One loomed out of the darkness, blinked its great eye at us and then mooed, like a cow searching for its lost calf.

Our course took us between the two forts before we headed farther south round the point of the Island to a bearing that would take us directly to Dieppe, over one hundred sea miles from Cowes.

As we came into the open sea, our speed increased in the forceful wind and the boat heeled over, bringing the lower side of the deck level with the sea and shipping several waves. John was taking the chance to get some sleep in one of the two bunks below and I had been at the tiller since dark as my eyes could cope with the dim light on the compass. By this time, the compass light had faded from orange to beige. I was afraid that if we went off course, the boat would turn over. Martin went below to get a torch —our only torch—and he just got back in time as the compass battery finally failed. Suddenly two huge waves hit us and drenched us and the boat. Martin was thrown over but still managed to keep the beam of the torch on the compass.

Luckily the course that had been worked out was also the best for the direction of the semi-gale. We were sailing at a speed that seemed greater than ski-ing, galloping, driving or flying, and which was partly accentuated by the groaning, creaking and slapping of all the rigging on the boat as we rocketed through the rough sea that hid its dangerous force in the inky darkness. Martin had been a navigator in a submarine, and found that a storm on the surface was a very different problem to what he had been used to.

I had sailed once or twice before but the only time I had ever sailed close to the wind, and then, in brilliant sunshine, I had felt a little doubtful about our safety as the angle of the boat increased. Now, with the tiller in my hands, and the boat like a bucking bronco under me as I sat against her with my feet braced against the opposite seat, I felt elated. The waves washed the deck and sprayed us from above as they broke over the boat. We cut through the noise of rough sea. Meeting the element of water with its weight of waves leaping against us from out of the darkness, I did not feel the clammy cold of my wet clothes in the excitement of handling the boat.

Martin decided to wake John, as we had too much sail for this rough weather, and neither of us had an idea how to reef the sail. My two hands were more than occupied with straining to keep the champing *Ayesha* on her course.

It seemed an age before John got his oilskins pulled over his clothes, but it must have been terribly difficult for him to dress while the boat was buffeted as it leapt over the crests and down into the troughs on our galloping way.

Eventually he poked his head through the hatch and exclaimed in horror when he saw the deck awash. He thought at first that the draining holes must be blocked, but actually the deck was too low on that side, for the sea water to have time to drain away.

He roped himself like a mountaineer to go forward to reef the sails. 'Brave man,' I thought as he disappeared into the breaking waves and spray to work his way forward along the slippery and tossing deck. I braced my feet more firmly and thanked my lucky stars that I was sitting securely wedged.

A voice floated back on the gale, 'Luff her off now.' 'What her off?' I asked myself, luckily guessing that I had to turn her bows into the wind to slacken the sail while he took a reef. After repeating this process four times, our speed slackened, but the boat seemed to be plunging more as the ratio of balance was upset by leaving the larger jib with the smaller area of reefed mainsail. This was put right by John and Martin who struggled forward with a smaller jib sail which made the boat much more manageable.

We could relax a little more with the decreased speed of sailing, so we joked about my lack of sailing jargon and for that matter lack of naval discipline. I told John that I had been very tempted to answer him back through the storm, 'Luff her off yourself, I'm busy steering!' Then as it was 3 a.m. the men took over and I went down to sleep for a bit.

I was very tired from the strain of three days jumping at the Great Yorkshire, followed by the hurried journey to Cowes and getting straight on to the boat without time for a proper meal during two days. In fact I was so tired that it needed all my determination and perseverance to remove my oilskins. I longed to drop on to the bunk just as I was. I struggled to make my numbed fingers undo buttons and remove my drenched socks and then discovered that the sea had found its way in between the joins of the oilskins and also down my neck. I sank down on the bunk, feeling damp and exhausted. Usually I am a light sleeper but in spite of the pitching of the boat and the noises of the sails buffeting and the timbers creaking, I felt myself sinking into a deep sleep—a sensation of sinking just as I once felt when fainting after it became too late to breathe deeply or take other anti-fainting precautions. In my sleep I could think and look down on myself sleeping and yet I had lost any power to summon myself back to wakefulness.

At 5 a.m. the other two came down to sleep. I buttoned on my wet oilskins and climbed through the hatch into the fine driving rain that had just started to drench the boat. The wind had dropped and the sea had changed from rough waves to towering rollers. I was quite glad to escape into the fresh dawn and leave the dark and heaving cabin.

Our course was the same and as I took the tiller from John, I thought I would ask him to let out the reefs, so that I could make full use of the slackening wind. One look at his tired and white face as he quickly disappeared made me refrain from asking. I wished later that we had more sail, because it became impossible to hold any course as the wind dropped. The rolling sea had the boat at its mercy as one moment we were perched on a mountain, and the next moment sliding down to the bottom of a green abyss, rather like descending into the dark valley of Lauterbrunnen from either Wengen or Mürren perched on the sheer mountains on either side. 'It must be awful below,' I thought as I sang some cheerful Mexican sambas—Twist would have been too close to reality!

A light shone in the distance and I wondered what it could be. It disappeared as we left the crest of the wave. The next time I looked I realized that the light was suddenly very near and seemed to be towering above us. It was a ship. There was no wind to make a tack, so I prayed that our paths would not coincide. The speed of the big boat took it across our bows well before there was any danger of our colliding, but it made me feel very small as it passed on its superior way, completely disgregarding us and without a person in sight on its many decks.

I thought of the great impression that the arrival of the Royal Yacht *Britannia* had made in Sweden, when she had sped through the maze of islands that mark the sixty miles of archipelago on the approach to Stockholm. As she lithely serpented her way down the narrow channel, not a person was to be seen on her except for our Queen who was standing on the bridge. It was as though the ship herself was obeying the royal command.

There was still no wind and less of a sea when we changed over and I went to get some more sleep. I did not think that the others looked very rested, judging by their colour, so perhaps I had been far better off coping with the rollers, the rain and the sudden appearance of the big ship.

I woke to find the boat quite still and enveloped in a terrible stench of diesel. The two men were trying to start the engine, and with my eyes shut, I listened to the various discussions on how to get a spark from the different parts of the engine that they were doctoring. After a long and trying time the engine condescended to cough off its sulkiness and rattle into action. I went to sleep again, asphyxiated with the fumes and envying the Kon-Tiki adventurers who were at least spared the noise and smell of engines. Next time I woke, the engine had stopped, to my great relief. Apparently we had nearly run out of fuel, as the people at Cowes had forgotten to fill the tins, so the last drop was being kept to help us manoeuvre in the harbour at Dieppe.

I ventured up into the fresh air and found the calm sea melting into the mist. It was not really foggy, as I could see the sky and yet there was no visibility at sea level. We could do nothing as we had no wind and no fuel. I did not particularly want to do anything, least of all to get on with some writing that I should have finished weeks before. It was amazing how quickly the day passed, doing nothing, except for some omelette cooking at supper time.

A little breeze began to play with the sails towards midnight, and half an hour later, between the sounds of Martin snoring, I heard the log, a little spinner that we were trailing to measure our distance travelled, start to turn. I felt energetic and took over from John, so that he could get some sleep.

Again the sea was completely changed and during our short voyage it showed more moods in different costumes than could ever be accredited to the best actress in the world. It was a silent sea and entirely flat although we were mid-Channel. With this new breeze, the boat cut its way through the water like a knife through soft butter. The tiller was as light in my hand as the steering wheel of a car with power steering, in fact I could not rest it against the weight of the water to keep a steady course. The lack of resistance gave the same effect as driving fast with power steering, when the car is too sensitive to be supported against the camber of the road.

We were moving in complete silence with no murmur of

slapping waves. Only the log, proving our mobility as it followed behind, made a soft swish as it turned. I was in a little world lit by our lamp; beyond this luminous circle the darkness dissolved into mist. There were no ships, no fog-horns and no sound. My eyes closed and I woke with a start to find to my relief that our route was unaltered. A plane passed high overhead so I thought that at least we must be on the right part of the sea with Dieppe lying on the Paris–London air route.

I shone the torch into the cabin to wake the others, feeling that I was a pig to disturb them, but I could not keep my eyes open any longer. Martin took over and I slept until I heard French voices greeting us. Some fishermen had appeared in the dawn.

There was a little early breeze but by mid-morning it dropped and the sun came out for the first time. I took the chance and had a swim. After the shock of diving in I held my breath until I could call nonchalantly, 'Come on, it's wonderful, warm as toast.' The others came reluctantly. John stayed in one moment and Martin for less!

We all felt cleaner and horribly healthy after our cold dip and by the time we had eaten a chicken, the breeze came back. We sailed all the afternoon and John and I became engrossed in serious conversation, discussing our views on life and religion. While we were exchanging our ideas on these unnautical subjects, Martin appeared out of the hatch, rubbing the sleep from his eyes and said, 'Hey, what's that, Holland or Spain?' We looked up and there was a great line of land ahead. I had been watching the compass and while we were talking John and I had not noticed!

The wind freshened and we scudded towards the cliffs and line of coast. The sailing 'pilots' described Dieppe in a dip

of the cliffs marked by a church and tower, with a radio
station on the left side and a prominent house on the right
cliff. We scanned the dip ahead with the glasses and the
description fitted exactly. We congratulated the navigator.
Closer to land, John with the glasses said in a worried
voice, 'I can't find the harbour, I think we'd better beat it
out to sea before we land on a bank or something. Then
we'll have a check up.' We about turned and made for a
buoy some way out, where we could identify our exact
position.

From the northeast an enormous thunder-cloud was bearing down on us and we wanted to know where we were
before the rain obliterated our view of the land. We
rapidly approached the buoy before the rain reached us.
We could hear that it was a whistler and John was scanning
the guide to find which buoy it was. 'Heavens,' he said.
'Has it a triangle on top?' 'I think so,' said Martin, a look
with the glasses confirming this. 'Well, we're right over
a dangerous wreck now, keep your eyes skinned to port and
starboard.' It was high tide so we must have had just
enough clearance, anyway now we knew where we were!

It was a little south of our destination so we turned up the
coast, and after passing another dip in the cliffs, with a radio
mast to the right and a prominent house to the left—but
again no harbour, we came to the third dip in the cliffs.
This time the line of harbour wall met our eye plus the
appropriate radio mast to the left, church and tower in the
dip and prominent house to the right, also rather a different
size of town, for this was Dieppe.

Through the heavy rain that by now was soaking us we
saw a rescue boat leave the harbour and come straight towards us. The French sailors tried to throw us a rope in

spite of our furious and indignant repeating of '*Non, allez vous-en.*' Why should we be treated as salvage? It is a well known way of extracting money from unsuspecting boats, and we were quite capable and competent to get into the harbour by ourselves. It turned out later that during a regatta that morning, one boat had been lost, and the salvage boat thought we might be the stray. Later it was discovered that the owner of the missing boat had found himself tailed off in the race and so called in on a friend farther down the coast for a little '*causerie*' and an '*apéritif*'.

The roughish sea and good breeze brought us past the harbour mouth, where I turned *Ayesha* into the wind as the men lowered the mainsail. Using only the jib, we sailed between the great walls of the entrance. Meantime, Martin and John were trying to start the motor without a spark of success. Eventually it relented and we chugged on one cylinder through the calm water of the sheltered harbour, past the moored ferry-boats and into the main basin. Apparently the yachting basin was the other side of a drawbridge. It was rush hour and a stream of traffic was using the bridge, so we had to wait for it to open. John was a little worried that our fuel would not last long, so as we took a turn round the harbour he tried to get her out of gear. Alas, the clutch had gone wrong and the gears were jammed. In a frustrating battle with the gears, suddenly something happened and the engine stalled. At that moment I heard the gendarme on the bridge shout: '*Après la camionette,*' and sure enough 'after the van', the traffic was stopped and the bridge opened. The engine would not start so John rushed forward and hoisted the jib again, then dashed back to have another go at the engine. The gendarme shouted and waved at us '*Allez, allez, vite!*'

[ 61 ]

There was hardly a breath of wind in the harbour and very slowly we drifted towards the bridge. Drivers were getting out of the cars and waving their arms at us so I called up 'Pardon, messieurs, il faut souffler un peu pour aller plus vite,' and I sat at the tiller blowing and puffing at the flapping sail. Eventually we floated through and the traffic started hurrying over the bridge again.

A French sailor rowed up to us with a mooring raft and helped us fix the boat. We talked to him about the modern construction of a loading shed on the far side of the basin, which had no supports on the harbour side for the concrete roof. He was a little doubtful about its stability and the safety of the people who worked in its shelter.

John and I climbed up the greasy harbour wall, and I staggered as I took my first steps on solid land. We went to a café and I asked John for Brigitte's telephone number. 'I thought you had it,' he said with surprise. I did not even know the name of the village where she lived, and as telephone numbers are listed in France, not under people's surnames, but under the name of their town or village, we were sunk. I only knew that she lived somewhere between Dieppe and Abbeville, but Abbeville is quite a distance away.

We tried the cafés, the police, the Syndicat d'Initiative, in fact anyone who was interested in our plight. A cousin of a waiter in a café knew someone of the same surname, but he proved to be no relation. We were in despair. We started to walk back to the boat to break the news to Martin. Suddenly I heard a familiar voice shouting 'Ola, chica!' It was Brigitte. She was dressed in a striped fisherman's shirt, and with her was John's wife, who had crossed the Channel by ferry-boat two days before. They had spent

[ 62 ]

most of the two days coming down to the harbour at intervals, hoping to intercept us.

We shouted for Martin who, I noticed, had also to get his land legs as he met the shore. We unloaded the boat, roping the heavy things carefully up to the road above, trying to keep them away from the oily wall. At a nearby hotel we met Brigitte's parents and cleaned up a little before driving the thirty-five miles back to their home. Until then I had forgotten that I had on three pairs of trousers, shorts, that I had put on after bathing that morning, dungarees to keep warm in the stiffish breeze and then twill trousers for protection against the thunderstorm!

That evening we joined the gay party of Brigitte's friends—French, Spanish and Italian, and we played the guitar far into the night. We laughed about our delayed arrival and imagined newspapers with headlines 'British rider missing at sea'. Luckily nobody had known of this week-end away and one of the best parts of sailing was the isolation from people, telephone or any form of publicity.

The next day Brigitte drove me to Calais where I only caught the paquet boat by a hoot of its blower, and arrived in England just in time to collect the horses and drive up to the White City for the International Horse Show.

The break had done good to both Flanagan and myself. We both arrived fresh at the White City and went into battle in great heart. Our team won the Nations Cup by only one fence, although Flanagan, Earlsrath Rambler and Nizefela had all jumped clear in the first round. Prince Philip presented our Olympic trio with engraved whips, for winning the bronze medal—I have carried that whip ever since. Flanagan won the National Jumping Championship from Alan Oliver on John Gilpin. Alan turned tables on

[ 63 ]

me to beat Flanagan by one-fifth of a second for the *Daily Mail* Championship in the last jump-off on Galway Boy. Turning to a fence in the timed jump-off, Flanagan had pulled a shoe off, which made him stumble and lose a valuable second. Without the shoe he still continued to jump clear. Alan had nothing to lose, and so 'riding a finish' from the start, he just made it.

This was the third time I had been pipped in this important event—in 1951 on Prince Hal by Foxhunter, and 1952 on Tosca by Tankard being the former defeats. However, both Prince Hal and Scorchin have won me the gold cup twice each, so only Flanagan can grumble that he has not got the credit—yet—for a fifth *Daily Mail* Cup.

If Flanagan had not had the complete rest while I went sailing for a few days, he would never have been able to bear the brunt of such a tough show. Prince Hal lamed himself and so poor Flanagan had to be called on for every performance, and with a few less last fences down, he could have established a great show record. The word 'if' is a very useful excuse for not winning. Horses and show jumping results are both strongly subjected to this small word.

# CHAPTER 7

# Sicilian Interlude

AT the end of the busy show jumping month of August, we went to British Timken, where we were always made so welcome by the late Sir John Pascoe. Flanagan obligingly won the big class with his stable pals Prince Hal and Carousel equal second to him. He also cleaned up on the Gamblers Stakes. Paul then set off on the sea journey to Rotterdam, where we were meeting up with the rest of the team. When the horses arrived, the rest of the team had already organized themselves in the tent provided for the horses. The night had to be spent finding odd bits of timber or benches that would help make barriers around the horses, so that they could lie down and rest from their journey.

These barriers were of necessity a fairly temporary measure, and only gave the horses enough room to lie down and just turn round. Two years later Flanagan was stabled between Mr Pollard and Grand Manan, my other two horses for Rotterdam. During the night he must have rolled and gone clean under the partition between his stall and Mr Pollard. Paul, in the morning, found the two chestnuts together in the one space, looking like Siamese twins with their heads side by side.

Another night in the same line of improvised stabling a horse jumped out of its box, landing on the foot of a sleeping groom. The grooms had their camp-beds in a line down the centre passage of the tent. That night the one loose horse encouraged two more to break out and chaos reigned for a time. Luckily no more damage was done, but our team groom was left very lame.

Although Flanagan won the Ladies Competition, the big question I had to ask him was in the Nations Cup. We were last to go in the second round. If we jumped another clear round, Great Britain would win the cup, if we made a fault, we would lose the cup. Flanagan pulled his weight again and we won by 2¼ faults from the Italians.

The funniest win we had there was when Alan Oliver on Galway Boy was paired with me on Prince Hal in the Jig-saw Stakes. In this team event, we both started at the same time and had to jump seven fences each of the fourteen fences in the arena. Our faults and final time counted for the winning prize. I galloped Hal around the seven perimeter fences to merit his team nickname of 'Hasty Harry'. Alan wiggled around the middle fences on Galway Boy—affectionately known as 'Weary Willy'—and we won.

So the jumping season continued, with one brief break when I went to meet my brother in Spain, and we drove back through the Pyrenees and the breath-taking gorges of the Tarn and its tributaries. Just for a week no one could contact me, and I was free to enjoy the late September sunshine gilding the beautiful countryside of central France, the wide views of the Cevennes and Auvergne, at a time too late for tourists and yet warm enough for cotton frocks.

October came and the last Horse Show of the English jumping season at Harringay. Then Prince Hal and Flanagan packed up their saddles and came with me to the Continent for the shows of Brussels, Paris and Sicily. I had been invited by the committees of Palermo and Catania and in spite of the long journey to Sicily, I had decided to go there because the horses would have the whole winter to rest.

At Brussels Prince Hal had won his third successive Puissance event at that show. To achieve this feat he had to jump seven rounds finishing over a 6' 11" wall and a spread fence. Those were the days when a Puissance could become a marathon event if two good horses continued to fight it out. Now the rule has been changed so that the jury can end the competition by letting horses divide, after the fourth or fifth jump-off. This does prevent a good horse having his nerve and heart broken by continually being overfaced.

'Le Jumping' at Paris gave Flanagan another international win to his credit. The competition was a fault and out over a large course of five-foot fences. We were third to go, it being a disadvantage to jump at the beginning of a speed class. However Flanagan, who needs impulsion for big fences, galloped twice round the course of twelve fences, within the time limit. After the last horse had jumped we were still two seconds ahead of Winkler, with Goyoaga third, showing that only the top horses could gallop over a course of this size. The prize of Napoleon's sabre was given by 'Miss United States' and, although one wondered if Napoleon would have agreed to his sabre going to Great Britain, he surely would have approved of the beautiful lady who made the presentation!

Earlier that day a 'Miss Jumping' had been chosen from the French ladies, and M. Jean de Faucon, the indefatigable 'speaker' at 'Le Jumping', had nearly found himself elected, but for three extra votes in favour of Mlle Jacqueline Luchaire!

Twelve years ago I told a Swiss friend who has rather kinky hair, the old joke that wogs began at Calais, little thinking that perhaps I might one day be termed as one myself. To an Italian, apparently, black men start south of Naples and Paul was warned of this before she started her journey to Sicily. Piero d'Inzeo's groom, Virgilio, told her of the danger of travelling south in the territory of the 'Moroccans'. He took the responsibility upon himself of seeing that she travelled unmolested by these 'foreigners' until they arrived in Palermo. There a disaster nearly overtook Prince Hal. Paul was leading him and riding Flanagan the four miles from the station to the stables when suddenly urchins rushed at them out of the dark and startled Hal. He lost his footing on the camber of the road and fell hard on to his side. He was very stiff the next day.

I stopped off at Rome on the way south. The first night after a visit to the theatre and a midnight supper of *pizza* in the old part of Rome, with an accompaniment of Italian songs sung to the guitar, we decided to go and investigate the activities of the leading national newspaper at an early hour. Rome was asleep, but the noise that greeted us as we entered the editorial office quickly dispelled any fears that we would be disturbing anyone. Reports were coming in from the uprising in Budapest and the Suez crisis, in code, out of code, by phone, by cable, by messenger-boy, and somehow everything was being sorted out into comprehensible reading material about the ghastly crimes and crises of that time.

About an hour or so later I was looking at some of the pictures around the walls of the office and I happened to remark on the beautiful views of Italy, depicted there in water-colour. 'I give the pictures to you,' I was astonished

Cantering past the last fence in the Team Event, a big parallel over water, the fence where Franco had run out and so eliminated our team

Aachen C.H.I.O. Galloping through the lake in a speed event

Speed in a White City event

Hickstead 1961. The Derby Trial Event down the easy side of the big bank

to hear the editor say. 'That's terribly kind, but you can't do that, besides I'm flying to Sicily tomorrow and I've already got excess baggage.' He was adamant. 'I wish to give them to you,' he assured me as he rose from his surroundings of reports, articles and urgent press material. He picked up his chair and stood on it as he unhooked each picture in turn, leaving me with eight large frames, four under each arm, and his bare office with eight light-coloured patches on the walls. I wondered if the same thing had ever happened in the editor's office of *The Times* at 4 a.m. I slunk out of the building with the loot bulging out from each side of me, and my companions laughing their heads off as the concierge gave me a most suspicious look.

So to Palermo, pictures and all, and as we flew in to land over the horseshoe bay of Sferracavallo I saw Monte Pellegrino to my left and to my right the wild hills, hunting ground and home of Sicily's most famous bandit Salvatore Guiliano, who was murdered at the age of twenty-eight. I was thrilled by my first evening view of this fascinating island, and when I stepped out of the plane the air was warm and scented, very different from the November nip and snow-tipped mountains I had just left at Rome.

Later I watched the sea shimmering as the light of the moon tickled the ripples in the calm of the night.

Near Palermo lay the Favorita Park, where Lady Hamilton lived for a time when Nelson had used Sicily as a centre for his activities. In this park the show was held, against a natural backcloth of the sheer cliff of Monte Pellegrino rising behind the bowl of the arena, which in turn was encompassed by Cyprus trees, banana trees, tropical shrubs and cacti of varying shades of green. Goethe defined this mountain as the finest promontory in the world.

In spite of the long and tough season that the horses had already endured, they seemed to appreciate leaving the approaching winter weather of London, Brussels and Paris, and the welcome warmth of these charming surroundings.

Prince Hal came through the show with flying colours and collected cups for competitions and for the best horse of the show. This was no mean feat when competing against the pick of the Italian horses and the other foreigners. From the crowd's point of view Flanagan was a highlight when he came in to receive a prize, with his head adorned by a coloured *pennacchio*, a pompom made of wools, such as those worn by all the best and smartest donkeys pulling the painted *carrettas*. These gay carts, decorated with scenes of crusades, battles and tales of jousting knights, together with the trappings on the donkey, are the pride of each peasant owner. It may cost them as much as £40 for their turnout, for the artistry that goes into the painting is a very specialized work, and is an art handed down the generations from father to son. A peasant may be poverty stricken, but the turnout of his *carretta* comes before food or clothing for his numerous family.

That morning I had searched the port for a maker of *pennacchios*, because they are only produced to order and then made with the colours chosen by the purchaser. At last I came to a room that opened on to the street, where an old man worked with leather, mending shoes, harness and odds and ends. He was surrounded by a swarm of children, as this seemed to be the family living-room. He told me that he would make a *pennacchio* for me and showed me the iron frame which he would bind with wools. I selected the colours for the pompom and asked how long it would take him to finish. He thought for a moment. I suppose

[ 70 ]

that living in an age of mass production, efficient salesman-
ship and American gadgets designed for quicker results
with less work, had not prepared me for his reply of '*Tre
settimane.*' Three weeks!—but I needed it that afternoon!
I tried to explain that this was the final day of the show
and the importance of honouring the Sicilian custom with
an international horse, in the final competition of Palermo.
With some lire to back my urgency he relented, and that
afternoon I had the most magnificent *pennacchio*.

Flanagan played his part and jumped a good round,
ensuring a place amongst the prize-winners. After his
round, Paul and I took him back to his stable and introduced
him to his head-dress. He was horrified at first. It
needed all of the half-hour before the end of the competition
and many carrots and apples to resign him to his fancy dress.
By the time we were called to the ring for the prize-giving,
he had decided that he indeed wore a fitting crown for a
prize-winner. He entered proudly, pointing his toes in his
parade walk. The other riders were very amused, but the
Sicilians were deeply touched and rose to their feet with
tears in their eyes. '*Brava! Brava!*' they cheered until
Flanagan thought that he was the best horse in the show,
stealing the thunder from Prince Hal. Paul then removed
his headdress before he got too conceited.

Each morning early, before changing for the show, I
had been out seeing many of the unique palaces, churches
and collections of art and sculpture in and around Palermo.
I had hired a brand-new Fiat 1,100. At the garage I
inquired as to the maximum speed for running in, and was
told that Fiats did not need running in. I took them at
their word and the car covered a lot of ground in a little
time. I went out to Monreale on a Sunday, and after Mass

in the cathedral, the great bronze doors were thrown open for a special procession. The sun streamed in, catching the gold and silver of the entire interior of Byzantine mosaics. It was as though a thousand lights had been switched on and the Old and New Testament scenes depicted in the mosaics seemed to come to life with the reflection of light dancing on the walls. In one mosaic panel, the sun made the water in the 'font' glisten as the Virgin Mary tested its temperature before bathing the baby Jesus. Another mass was being celebrated in the Capella Palatina, and the beauty of the more petite and perfect mosaics of this royal chapel blended into the music of the service. The palace and chapel were in the care of Carlo, who showed me around his precious charges, lovingly describing their wonders and ancient history in his lilting musical voice. Italian, spoken by a Florentine such as Carlo, sounds more like poetry than prose and nearer to music than speech.

We finished our tour by looking over Palermo from the palace balcony. I asked Carlo about the handsome statue of a knight on his horse below in front of the palace. 'Oh, that is Philip V. It used to be Philip IV, but he was in bronze and had to be melted down for a war, then he was replaced by Philip V who had himself done in màrble so that he could not suffer the same fate!' I looked at a rusty cannon nearby, and wondered if it was all that remained of poor Philip IV.

From the Arabic, Byzantine and Norman churches of Palermo, I was taken to the Greek and Doric temples of Agrigento. Time is ignored, and these great works of 600 B.C. will defy the mortality of passing generations for centuries to come. Jupiter, Hercules, Castor and Pollux— these are all names of immortals whose man-made temples of twenty-five centuries ago are a humbling reminder that great achievements are not confined to this modern age. I walked around the great colossi, the stone giants that supported the weight of the temple roof, and I decided that I would get a very stiff neck if destiny made me a Caryatid. The gentlemen who also helped support the roof were called Telamones and they could be identified by their only clothing of a sheepskin.

From an atmosphere of another age, where legends and myths become quite credible, the busy city of Catania came as a shock. I was not ready to return to modern life, and apart from the duties of show jumping, I was glad to get away to Taormina described as '*Un amore*'—a love of a town. Built on the hillside above the sea, and below the ancient Greek Theatre it has still an old-world attraction in spite of the tourist lures in every corner. The streets are gay with the hand embroidered skirts and drawn-thread embroidered blouses, once taught to the local people by an English woman, and since then this work has become a speciality. Perhaps I saw Taormina at its most peaceful and best, for the summer visitors had gone and the winter residents had not yet arrived.

As I drove along the coast that night, the clear sky was full of stars. Occasional vivid flashes of lightning on the horizon were answered by the little blinking lights of the night fishermen, who were spearing the big fish when they came into the beam of their lamps.

From the auditorium of the Greek Theatre at Taormina, I looked across the ancient stage to snow-capped Etna in the distance. The next day we explored the volcano's black lava fields and cheekily climbed down into some of its craters.

Before I left this island of legend, I visited Syracusa and stored away many vivid memories. There I found places which gave the authentic background to stories that I had often thought about in imagination, such as the fountain of Arethusa, the ear of Dionysius, the caves where Christians had been herded and left to die—then the catacombs that were said to stretch nearly back to Catania, and had never been fully explored. Near the entrance to the catacombs were the ruins of an old church, with the framework of a lovely rose window in its one standing wall. Below in the crypt, where the original church had been built, St Paul had preached during the three days he had stayed at Syracusa. In the museum I was shown Neolithic implements and beautiful Corinthian pottery of the seventh and sixth centuries B.C. with figures of black on red or red on black.

The reward for the Greek athletes of the sixth and fifth centuries B.C. interested me. Instead of receiving a cup, a statue was made of the winners of gymnastic and sports events. Many of these are perfectly preserved now, showing the various activities of the Greek youths. I wondered if this would be a good idea for present-day competitions, but now with the new style of sculpturing I fear that the people of 2,000 years hence would be misled into believing that present-day athletes had no stomachs, twisted limbs and very little brain, in fact, occasionally only a trace of neck with no head!

Pauline with Prince Hal and Flanagan had an interesting journey in a slow train consisting almost entirely of the show horses travelling to Catania. Most of these were Italian, with their grooms, some being young army boys. The train often slowed up for no apparent reason which gave the young Italians a chance to leap out of the horse wagons and raid the nearest citrus plantation. It was a relief from the boredom of the journey.

In one orange grove they were met by an angry farmer with a gun who fired on them. Undeterred for long they again took advantage when the train came to a halt near a high wall guarding an orchard. Just by the wagon, where Paul and her charges were watching with interest, the wall was broken. The men streamed over this breach in the defences. At that moment the train gave a 'peep' and started moving again. The men poured back over the broken bit of wall, laden with lemons. Paul having the nearest open door received the bulk of the fruit while the grooms dashed for their wagons as the speed of the train increased. Peace was restored once more as the sound of the tickety-tock increased, but Paul was horrified to find that she had not only two chestnut horses but also a few hundredweight of green lemons in a huge rattling pile around the open door.

A thunderstorm at Catania transformed it into Venice, and washed out the show for a day. This did not worry Flanagan who loves mud. His competition was the Gamblers Stakes which is our speciality. He must be a good mathematician, or perhaps he trusts to luck. We were near the beginning of the competition and got a score of 640 points clear over the biggest fences, including three enormous jumps of parallel poles and a 5′ 6″ straight wall, all in 60 seconds. I then waited on tenterhooks while the d'Inzeos brought out horse after horse, finishing with Merano. The 'ace' card of parallel poles was his undoing and so the Union Jack stayed at the top of the flagpole.

Paul and the horses had a long and cold journey home, with ten days of jolting in trains from Sicilian warmth to the late November discomfort of our latitudes. The train never halted by a water-tap, and Paul had to melt ice on her tiny meta stove, so that the horses could drink.

I had an easier time flying home from Sicily and our route took us over the volcanoes from Etna to Stromboli and Vesuvius. Clouds then closed over Italy, leaving us alone with the sky. The weather was clear by the time we reached the Alps and as we flew round the Italian side of the Matterhorn, I saw ski tracks over the Theodul Pass. I had always longed to ski over to Italy from Zermatt, an ambition I realized four months later.

A few hours after arriving in London, with little time to prepare for the importance of the occasion, I found myself with many famous and interesting people waiting for an investiture at Buckingham Palace. The inside of the palace was more impressive than I had ever imagined, with the wonderful pictures, and exquisite furnishings.

This exciting occasion was shared with me by my brother, who had just been instituted into his first parish at Belhus Park. Also my uncle, Lt.-Col. Gordon Smythe, who had first persuaded our family to make our life in Gloucestershire. They saw the Queen present me with the O.B.E., and Her Majesty had read of our Sicilian progress and knew Prince Hal and Flanagan from seeing them jumping at some shows. Flanagan had made his gallant effort at Stockholm in front of our Queen.

From these regal surroundings, I went on, that evening, to Wormwood Scrubs—to lecture to a most intelligent and attentive audience of prisoners.

# CHAPTER 8

# Flanagan on Ice

FLANAGAN and Prince Hal had earned a full rest from their busy year. While they were grazing the Gloucestershire banks, my New Year started with a resolution to jump a fence of at least 6' that morning. This crazy idea was soon made possible by my Spanish hosts producing their Anglo-Arab horse and a selection of jumps. I wondered if I had been wise to speak but without wasting further time I carried out my resolution. It was an unexpected beginning to the year, jumping a French-bred horse called Epinard, over a 6' wall in Spain, but I had arrived in Barcelona the night before, officially in order to finish some writing and unofficially to get a week-end's ski-ing in the Pyrenees. As well as the writing being accomplished, a plan was formed to go to Davos in March for the Horse Show and some ski-ing.

My own Carousel came from England with Pauline and we met up with Epinard, who had been leased to me, in Davos to try this Swiss sport of jumping horses on the snow. Our horses had never before had so many screws put in their feet to stop them slipping, then we had to fill their hooves with wax to prevent the snow from balling in their feet. They seemed to settle down to their jumping with plenty of confidence, in fact more confidence than I felt, as we were jumping on the ice-rink sprayed with snow. However, all went well and Carousel won the Prix du

Parsenn. With this prize, the committee gave me a lovely black blouse with the special hand-embroidery of the Engadine. My only trouble was that I could not thank anyone for their kindness and congratulations because I had lost my voice, due to 'flu and a temperature. I could not have chosen a better place to have a throat and chest infection, so with the experts and experience from the many sanatoriums, I was soon put right.

Ski-ing on the Parsenn and the Brahma Buel, after the jumping had finished each afternoon, helped to get me fit before an energetic week at Wengen. While the horses travelled from Davos to Turin, I broke the journey in the Oberland to get some more ski-ing.

It was nearly the end of the ski-ing season, but I arrived in time to join the last *ski schule* party. This great occasion was marked by my receiving a prize of a cork with a bear carving on it. I was the winner of the Slalom race (Class four!) certainly among the greatest achievements of my life.

Oskar, who was head of the *ski schule*, and a great climbing guide, took me to the Jungfraujoch. From there we climbed the Mönch, a mountain of 4,105 metres lying between its two companions the Jungfrau and the Eiger. I had never climbed before but I soon learnt the determination needed to make oneself go on at that height. Every time I stopped for breath, the after-effects of 'flu made me cough, and coughing wasted more valuable breath. I felt quite philosophic about the sheer sides dropping away from our ridge of soft snow. It made me wonder if this was the reason for the guides always wearing leather sides to their dark glasses, like blinkers on a horse, to avoid catching sight, out of the corner of the eye, of a ghastly drop below. I just looked down at the next place for my foot, as my glasses had no sides. Wherever I wanted to step, the place seemed made for the wrong foot. At this height, problems are more complicated to sort out.

We were roped, so when the snow gave under my foot and I slipped off the ridge, there was a comforting tug to prevent my complete disappearance below. Each time I looked up, I thought the summit must be just five minutes away. Each time, this summit turned out to be just another shoulder of mountain, and as I climbed on to it, another snowy and rocky ridge stretched away above me. At last Oskar said, 'Well done, what d'you think of it?' I still thought we had farther to go, until I realized that the next ridge was going *downhill* and we were really on top.

Mist was swirling round the Jungfrau and Eiger, but somehow our peak was clear. We could see Wengen and the land stretching away to beyond Bern, but the wind made my eyes cry, when looking in that direction. The Matterhorn had been obscured by mist and we decided to go straight on down.

My knees developed automatic movements going down, and I was glad to rest for a moment while three Swiss, who had come up to the Jungfraujoch in the same train as us, passed us on a narrow ridge. They were still on their way up, and they took some photos of us with my camera. We soon arrived down to where we had left our skis, and I gladly strapped them on to stop myself sinking more than knee-deep in the soft snow, at every step. The ski-ing was easy back to the Jungfraujoch, past the great chunk of icefall sitting on the glacier, that had been used in a French film as the summit of Annapurna.

We picked up the extra haversack and then I found to my horror that we were ski-ing down on breakable crust. I am no expert skier and my skis were faster than Oskar's, also my knees were weak after the climb. It seemed impossible to keêp behind him or to control my disobedient skis when they broke through the thin layer of ice into the softer snow underneath. Conditions became easier as we went on and instead of zigzagging, we took the gentler slope straight with skis together. I was awed by the magnificence of the great open space of glacier snow at the cross-roads of the Concordiaplatz where the three glaciers meet and continue together down the Aletschgletscher. While I was admiring the view, I carelessly missed the track and the next moment I was upside down in the soft snow. At first I found it a wonderful rest to stay exactly as I had fallen. Then as the snow began to penetrate I started my efforts to get up again. Anyone who has tried to get out of deep soft snow with a rucksack strapped on their shoulders and knees as tired as mine were, will guess the trouble I had. Once back on the track, I firmly kept my eyes to the front and eventually arrived safely at the base of the rock leading to the Concordiahut.

Leaving our skis, we had quite a rock climb to get to the hut. When the hut was first built, it was level with the glacier, but since then the glacier has receded and has left the hut perched up on the rock above. In fact it is quite excusable to rope for the ascent! One friend had confided to me that she had made her guide rope her, when she had to visit the W.C. along a slippery and precipitous path several yards from the hut itself. To be blown off that path would be a sad end after surviving many other hazards.

In the hut, we took our turn at the stove to melt some snow for water and then heat up some *bouillon* and *ravioli*.

There were Italians, Germans, French and Swiss and myself representing the home country, all making use of the facilities offered by the hut. Some of them left at dawn but we waited for the sun, and then skied down the crisp and glistening icy snow surrounded by towering peaks against a clear blue sky.

The crevasses were very open for March, and we wound our way between most impressive cracks and chasms as the glacier turned in its course, to face the distant Matterhorn.

A fortnight later, after jumping at Turin, I was ski-ing down the Theodulgletscher around the Matterhorn, and could see the mountains marking the Aletschgletscher.

A vague arrangement had been made to meet at Brig in the afternoon of the day after the Turin Show had finished. I managed to leave all my luggage at the stables and say good-bye to the many friends made during the show, and caught the train. I was half asleep until we arrived at Domodossola, but there, the Italian customs officers boarded the train. With only a guitar, a toothbrush and a spare pair of socks and gloves, I did not excite much suspicion, but within two minutes one good-looking young officer came back into the carriage.

'Are you going ski-ing?' he asked.

'Well,' I replied, 'I was doing two days on the glaciers en route for home.'

'Where is home? Are you Italian?'

I laughed because I was trying my Castilian Spanish with a few Italian words and the Italian tone of voice thrown in.

'No, I'm English.'

'Have you been here long?'

'Just a week at Turin.'

'Ah,' he said, 'there was an English girl at the Horse Show

in Turin this week. I saw the account in the papers, do you know her?'

We established identities and he immediately asked me why I was not married, followed by a proposal. 'For,' he said, 'obviously you like Italy and also like the mountains.'

Our conversation was interrupted by his having to leave the train and go on a mountain patrol.

As the train entered the Simplon tunnel, another man came into my carriage. The conversation followed the route of the first one, and before the train was out of the tunnel, I was told there was a nice church at Brig, and a marriage ceremony could quickly be arranged.

I did not acquiesce with this suggestion as I did not fancy a life of continuous customs duties in the Simplon tunnel.

At Brig, just when I was wondering where and how to escape, Oskar and the others of the party met me. That night we were eating *Raclette*, delicious thin slices of roasted cheese and washing it down with *Fendant*, the local wine, in Zermatt.

Herman Geiger is the great Swiss pioneer of mountain flying. He developed the technique of fitting on to his little plane skis that could be lowered in the air after a normal take off, so that a landing can be made on snow. Once the success of this scheme had been established, he was able to organize mountain rescues for injured climbers and skiers. Gradually he found that there was also a very remunerative trade in flying lazy skiers on to remote mountains, so that they could get the full benefit of a glacier descent, without spending the time and energy needed to climb up to the head of the glacier.

We took advantage of this and early next morning we took the first train to Riffelberg and waited for Geiger to pick us up in his plane, and fly us to the top of the glacier. Eventually we heard the throb of the two planes as he and a friend flew over the mountains from Sion and landed on the little patch of snow where we were waiting. Oskar and I went up first, one in each plane, and as soon as we had taken off, I could see the village of Zermatt far below. The next moment we were circling at the base of the Matterhorn and then up, until we landed and skied on the plane's skis lowered for landing, to the top of the Theodul Pass.

On the way up, I had seen people climbing the long glaciers, from where we had been, a four-hours' walk to the top. I did not feel guilty at doing it the easy way as I only had two days to spare.

After ski-ing down to Cervinia we spent the afternoon in the sun, for my part recovering from the hectic week's horse show. Then next morning early, we were up on the glaciers again. We started the long 'shuss' down, and my skis carried me away in front. I felt in wonderful form and exhilarated by the beauty of the surroundings. There was a profound peace on the expanse of glacier. It was a joy to be away from crowds and away from mechanized transport. A little plane buzzed tourists around the Breithorn and Monterosa and I pitied them. I had the righteous feeling of being alone and aloof on the glacier.

The others joined me and we continued to the sheer rocky cliff leading to the Matterhorn. The silence was interspersed by the rattle of falling stones. The sun had loosened the frozen rocks and I was glad that I did not have to climb the cliff.

The morning tour of wonderful ski-ing, and then a lovely walk down through the pinewoods where the snow had gone, brought us back to Zermatt. At 5 a.m. next morning I had to get up and leave by train, because my plane went from Geneva at midday. That morning, six Germans started the same tour that we had just done and were overtaken by a snowstorm. Their ski-ing holiday ended in tragedy with two of them dying of exposure. Such are the risks of glaciers and weather and thus the mountains retain their respect.

In London the customs officials asked me how long I had been away, with only the socks, gloves and guitar to declare. They looked a little askance when I told them it was nearly a month since I had been in England. Someone remarked, 'We'll be seeing you on TV tomorrow, won't we?' I had nearly forgotten that we had a programme booked for the next day.

Waking up at home in the morning, I thought 'There's a lot of green on the mountains, the snow must have melted during the night.' Suddenly I remembered that it was our Miserden yew tree against the grey dawn of early morning. The phone rang—Yes—I was at home. Soon I was at work with the horses and the television staff, and our programme was prepared for the afternoon. The weather was kind and everything went off as it should, in spite of frights with the radio mike during rehearsal, such as the battery failing, or my forgetting to talk into it while I was jumping, because I was enjoying myself so much back at the old sport! Here was a job where I felt really at home. Why go risking one's neck on glaciers?—but I would not have missed one moment of it.

Flanagan enjoyed his winter spent out on the banks, protected by his woolly coat, but he got bored towards the end of his long holiday and was delighted when we fetched him in to start work. During March he went out for long

Speeding over a bank to win at the Barcelona C.H.I.O.

Over the open water in the Hickstead Derby

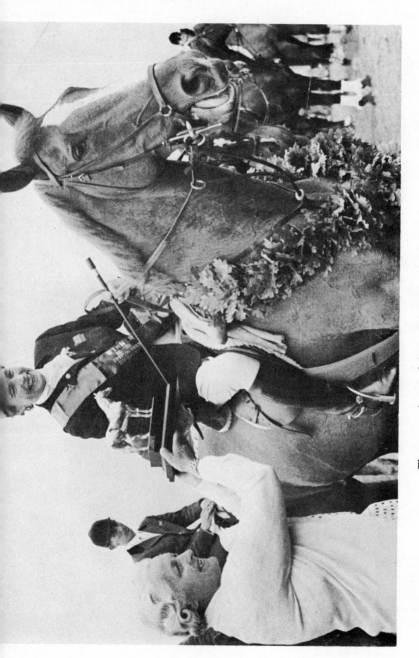

Flanagan, winner of the 1962 Derby, eats his laurels

White City Royal International Horse Show. Mr Robert Hanson stands by Flanaga
who had won the Saddle of Honour for the best individual horse through the sho
and together with Scorchin the Loriners Cup for the best two horses in the sho

walks to get his muscle back and his legs hardened. He would look longingly at the gates and fences, hoping that he would be allowed to jump one. By the end of April he was longing for competition and at Badminton proved himself ready to win the Area International Trial for Gloucestershire. A month later he collected the Area International Trial for Devonshire as well.

Before the White City had come round, we had already been overseas to Dublin Spring Show, Paris, and Spa. Although Flanagan had notched up successes at the first two shows, it was at Spa where he helped me win the first Ladies European Championship to be held.

There was an interesting diversion on the train from the Turkish grooms who were travelling with their team horses leaving Paris. Once the horses were loaded, the Turkish equivalent to a sergeant-major got all his groom boys on the platform with a couple of tubs of water between them. They then had to strip, scrub themselves and rinse their clothes in the two tubs, before boarding the train and sleeping with the horses, and presumably their wet clothes, in transit. Meanwhile, the sergeant-major had a whole wagon to himself, where he had his carpet, his bed, a table and chair, and the suitable face to go with these luxuries.

The Turkish men sleeping in the wagons with their horses were undeterred by the danger of resting so close to the feet of their charges. One Turk may have felt that the quarters were not roomy enough, for Paul found him trying to get into her wagon, when the train had stopped on an open bit of line. She did not relish the thought of his company for the following twelve hours, if the train did not stop again. With a superhuman effort she threw him off balance and out of her wagon; at that moment, the train gathered speed again and she still wonders if he caught hold of one of the few wagons on the tail of the train. Otherwise he may still be wandering amongst the sugar-beet in the north of France.

Once at Spa we got down to work again, and the rules for the championship meant that the four finalists had to change horses, and ride each horse in the last event. The rules have been altered since then and horses do not have to be ridden by other competitors.

Flanagan survived the ordeal although he was a little anxious about his mouth for a short time afterwards. It was Prince Hal who clinched the championship for me in a final jump-off, but he had his mouth cut in the process. His lip was scarcely healed by White City week. Flanagan helped our team win the Nations Cup that year and Prince Hal took the final White City Championship, for the second time, the *Daily Mail* Cup. This was his last international competition. Next time Flanagan went abroad he had another companion.

We went to America that autumn with Flanagan and Private Enterprise, a horse that had been lent to me for the tour while Prince Hal was ill. Paul and I heard that Hal had died, while we were jumping in New York.

We had flown the horses to America, as there was only a week to get them there, straight from the last night at Harringay. Travelling by air is much less tiring for the horses but also costs much more than the sea freight.

After finishing the shows, the horses returned by sea, because they would be rested all the winter. The Atlantic winter weather was unkind on this crossing and the ship ran into a full gale. Eventually it was so bad that the captain decided to turn round and run before the gale.

[ 86 ]

Flanagan was in a small covered crate which was fastened on the deck. Paul could open a trap-door in the front to put in food and water. She could also crawl in to straighten his front bandages and the front of his rug, but she could not get at his hind quarters. During the gale Flanagan managed to wedge himself comfortably enough in the crate, while horses in bigger boxes suffered more, being thrown from side to side.

One morning Paul went to feed him as usual, but, when she opened the trap-door, there was his tail! It was un-believable that he could have turned around, in so little space, but there he was. She could not get him out of the crate, because there was no protection on the open deck for a frightened horse with the boat pitching as it hit the great waves. Hoping that the smell of food would give Flanagan the incentive to contort himself once more and finish up the right way round, she put his feed under his tail, and closed the trap-door. Imagine her relief when she returned later, and found an empty bucket and his muzzle instead of his tail to greet her.

Our 1958 season started with Flanagan's first experience of jumping on snow at Davos in March. He was astounded with all the whiteness around and he was completely dazzled by the bright sun sparkling on the snow. His eyes watered and he had to blink them quickly or keep them half closed. Paul and I discussed the practicability of making dark glasses for him. There was a snag to this, because in competitions a rule prevents the use of blinkers or hoods, and glasses might have come into this category.

The first time we took them out for exercise we put wax into the horses' feet and screwed big studs into their shoes to stop them slipping. I was riding Flanagan along the road, with Paul following on Carousel. Suddenly Flanagan's eyes shot out on stalks and he nearly fell over with fright. He had just seen a man with feet seven foot long. I had forgotten that Flanagan had not seen skis before and the innocent skier poling along the snowy path could not imagine what all the fuss was about!

Paul had a worse experience on the journey from Davos to Turin. The wagon in which she was travelling with the horses was taken off the train at Milan, to be put on a branch line to Turin in the morning, Instead of being left in the usual goods yard, the wagon was put on a turntable and started to descend to an underground sorting place. She did not know what was happening and so slid back the big door a little so that she could see out. At that moment the wagon passed the lift control box and the men working there saw a girl looking out.

When the wagon was parked below, Paul laced the slightly open door with a rope, in case anyone should try and get in during the night. She went to sleep but suddenly was awoken by Flanagan snorting. He is quite a good watchdog and she knew something was wrong. There inside the wagon was a big brawny Italian. She was all alone at the end of this underground parking cul-de-sac. She was amazed how he had got through the rope lacing without waking her, but in a bound she was out of her sleeping-bag and through the rope. Wisely she removed the rope from the outside, so that the man would not stay in the wagon. Then she ran over to the lights at the exit where she could be heard if she shouted. Eventually the man left and she could go back and rope the door shut from the inside. Since then, when travelling through that way, she has hidden herself quietly in the wagon, while on the lift, so that the men do not realize that anyone is travelling with the horses.

Paul was one of the first girl grooms to travel abroad, and as a pioneer she had to establish that she could take more responsibility and keep the horses twice as efficiently as most of the foreign male grooms. At the present time it is easier with so many girl grooms in charge of horses, but then it was unique. Many foreign grooms who travel with international show jumpers now come to her for advice, and acknowledge her as the top person where experience in the caring and travelling of show jumpers is concerned.

# CHAPTER 9

# Paul to the Rescue

MY horses deserved a winter's rest after the Olympic year and once the autumn shows were over the time came to turn them out. They had already grown fairly woolly coats, which would protect them from the winter weather. Cold does not affect horses nearly as much as the wet. For this reason we put grease on the horses' backs before they are turned out, so that the rain will run off without penetrating the coat over their loins. All the jumping season the horses are very well groomed and so by the end of the year there is not enough natural grease in their coats to give them full protection against the elements.

Flanagan had rounded off his season by being second in the leading show jumper of the year at Wembley to Ted Williams on the great little grey Pegasus. Dawn Wofford and I had then taken our two Olympic horses Hollandia and Flanagan, accompanied by Scorchin, on to Brussels and Liege. My two won me the ladies Carven prize at both shows with a highlight at each. In Brussels Flanagan put his best foot forward to win the 'choose your points' event. There were twelve fences set for the course, with a wall at 5′ 7″ and an oxer at 5′ 3″ for the maximum of 100 points. We cleared fifteen fences within the minute allowed and scored 1,030 points. This was the first time that four figures had been reached in this competition and the cup that we won is in Paul's keeping as a souvenir. The Belgian newspapers said that I was probably always top in arithmetic at school and that I never lost a 'flea of ground' (*un pouce de terrain*) but they did not mention that Flanagan could also put two and two together. Raimondo d'Inzeo on Posillipo, the Olympic individual gold medal combination, came second with 940 points. This show was the last appearance of Halla, the great mare who won Hans Winkler three Olympic gold medals. She was retired after winning the Grand Prix de Bruxelles.

The Puissance in Liege gave Scorchin a chance to give me the second highlight of the trip. With the wall at 6′ 7″ out of heavy sand, three horses were still clear, Bacchus, Kilrush and Scorchin. The fifth round was over the wall at 6′ 10″ (2·10 metres) and a spread 5′ 11″ high and 6′ 3″ wide, and Bacchus again went clear. Scorchin, next to go, calmly jumped this height as well. Kilrush hit the wall and so was third. Neither Alwin Schockemohle nor I wished to face our horses with another round that night, especially as the prize was not a very important one with a first of £35 and second of £30 or its equivalent in francs. I was delighted that Scorchin could jump 2·10 metres, a height that I had only cleared before on Harry Llewellyn's Kilgeddin and on Prince Hal, who jumped 2·20 metres.

November saw me at home again and Flanagan having his annual leg blister, to take away any lumps and bumps from the season's jumping. Meanwhile, we wanted to put Scorchin and Telebrae out together on a nearby bank. Flanagan was to join them about a week later. When we got to the field, Paul let Telebrae go and he immediately put down his head to start eating. I slipped off Scorchin's headcollar saying, 'Whoa, son,' but he was not listening. He had spotted a chestnut pony in another field in the distance, and thinking that it was Flanagan, he whinnied and jumped the dividing fence of the fields. He stopped as soon as he landed and did not go to join the pony. His face wore a comic look as he turned to see what I was going to do about it. I clambered over the fence and through the mud and put on Scorchin's headcollar again. I had to lead him quite a long way around to get back to the field where Telebrae was still eating. The next time I loosed him, Paul had stationed herself at the only jumpable place in the fence. He stood for a moment sizing up the possibility of avoiding Paul and then he turned for an enormous place with oxer wire on each side. This he cleared easily, stopped and looked back at me. I was furious about the danger of his taking on barbed wire, but I had to fetch him back again. I nearly lost a gumboot in the mud as I squelched through the ditch and then the barbed wire nicked a neat triangle out of my trousers. Scorchin waited for me and then plodded patiently back to the other field.

The third time I loosed him I thought that he would have had enough of his game. Not a bit of it. This time he not only jumped the fence again but encouraged Telebrae to go with him! Paul and I went to fetch them both and were relieved when the last time we let them go in the correct field, they settled down to graze the grass and behave themselves for the rest of the winter.

I went away to Australia and New Zealand while the horses had their holiday. It was nearly the end of May when I returned home, but I had written to Paul to ask her to get the horses up from grass about a month before I returned. She was going to give them road work to harden their legs and get their muscles ready for faster work. Telebrae was the first one that she brought up. Flanagan and Scorchin were put into our jumping paddock for a few days to wait until the blacksmith had time to shoe them.

Telebrae's feet were already prepared for road work and so Paul took him for a ride. Returning home with him she suddenly saw Flanagan silhouetted against the sky. She could not believe her eyes, as there is no skyline to that paddock. On closer inspection she found that he had jumped up over the wall that surrounds the Miserden reservoir. He had found some very choice untouched grass on the top and he looked down on Paul like the King of the Castle. Paul reinstated him to the paddock and told him that he had only one more day's holiday, and that it was about time he started to work again.

The next day a hunting friend of mine who farms near us was disturbed by some men. They said that two horses had galloped up the road in front of their car and did they belong to him?

Our friend went out and acquired the horses off the road, but said that he knew nothing about them. He then started to phone around to see who had lost some horses. Whilst he was phoning, stories came in about other people who had also had these horses galloping past them during the morning.

Eventually he was advised to get in touch with a local farmer who does occasionally buy and sell horses. However, the dealer had not lost any animals and our friend was still at a loss. The next morning he thought that he would ring Paddy, just in case we could suggest where the two rough-looking beasts might belong. He started apologetically saying that he did not expect that we had lost any horses, but he had got these two cart-horses off the road and could not find a home for them.

Paddy does not deal with the horse department and did not think that we had lost any of our valuable animals. Luckily she was a little suspicious, knowing the sense of humour of some of the characters, and so she asked what the horses looked like. She was told that they were both boys and one was a very hairy chestnut with collar rubs on his shoulders, obviously got from working in harness. The other was an even hairier bay with a mane a foot long standing straight up on end. Both the horses were covered with mud and had tails to the ground. Paddy immediately called Paul to the phone!

Paul and Sheila were having breakfast, just prior to fetching Flanagan and Scorchin in from their winter's rest. Everyone bundled into the van after the phone call and rushed to our neighbour's farm. There they were greeted by Flanagan and Scorchin, who had smiles on their faces and were looking forward to plenty of attention again having had their final holiday spree.

Poor Paul gratefully thanked our friend for phoning, saying that she would have had kittens if she had gone up to the jumping paddock after breakfast and found thousands of pounds' worth of Olympic horses had vanished.

Paul and Sheila put headcollars on the two truant boys and rode them bareback along the road to home. Paul said to our friend as she left the farm, 'They may not look much now, but you come and see them in a month and you won't recognize them!' I was on the other side of the world and completely unaware of these happenings.

The collar mark on Flanagan's shoulder had been caused by a New Zealand rug that he had been turned out in when he first stayed out at night after being blistered.

The long rest had done them good and, when I got home, they won with three clears each at the first show where I jumped them. Bob Hanson was the President of Wickersley and so I nominated Flanagan as the winner of the competition. It was a satisfactory day for us and I was delighted to be back on my own horses again.

Our first C.H.I.O. that season was at Copenhagen in the gay atmosphere of the friendly Danes. The horses acquitted themselves well and Flanagan won a competition before coming second to Scorchin in the Grand Prix. This final win also gave me the Coupe Carven and I hoped that my handsome Viking boy-friend Absolum, who sits proudly on a bronze horse in the city, would be justly proud of me. I had first been introduced to him by Lis and Finn Hartel four years before, when I was on my way back from a lecture tour in Sweden. Lis Hartel had won the bronze medal for dressage at Stockholm in spite of her partial paralysis from polio.

From Denmark we travelled to Aachen in Germany. Both horses jumped consistently and Flanagan won me the ladies competition. This lovely prize of six silver mugs I was able to add to the six that I had won on Mr Pollard for the same event in 1958. The competition that Flanagan enjoys most at Aachen is the speed event where the horses have to gallop through the lake. He grins all over his face as the water tickles his tummy while he splashes along. He enjoys it almost too much, because in another competition with a proper water jump, he just popped straight into it and hit his nose on the far bank.

Before we went to Deauville for the Ladies European Championship, Flanagan won an event at Hickstead. Then we left for France without Paul. It was the first time she had not travelled abroad with my horses since the 1949 season. The reason was that she had broken some bones in her foot, not from Scorchin treading on it, but from an accident in the yard while travelling as a passenger on a motor-scooter. A New Zealand friend, Jenny Dalby, who was staying with us, was able to come with the horses to help me.

The weather could not have been more unkind to us at Deauville. A gale blew all the time, making the course-builders' job one of not only constructing the fences, but then tethering them to the ground and seeing that no jump was put in the direct path of the wind. Apart from the wind, there was rain. Some of the most penetrating rain imaginable soaked us through and stung our faces as it was blown horizontally at us in the teeth of the gale. In the evening, arriving back at our lovely hotel, soaked and shivering after each day's competitions, we could not profit from our proximity to the sandy beach.

Scorchin and Flanagan, being used to wet conditions, were quite unperturbed by the weather. There were altogether four competitions and they won all of them. Only three counted for the Ladies European Championship but, as a concession, the ladies were also allowed to compete against the men in the Test competition. This Scorchin won, having already been equal first in the other Test competition for the Ladies, and winning the first event. It was Flanagan who won the final Ladies event after two rounds followed by a jump-off against my friend Michèle Cancre.

Jenny certainly had a hundred per cent success on her first trip with British horses, but she had got very wet in the process. If Paul had insisted on coming too, the plaster on her broken foot would have melted away in the rain. However, I was sorry that Paul had not been able to share that show with me.

Behind the scenes and before the horse enters the ring, there is so much work to do, and real care and attention are needed from the person who is in charge of a horse. Arriving in foreign countries, with new kinds of grasses in the hay mixture and new types of oats for the main feed, a horse can get stomach troubles which must immediately be treated, or it may die of colic. Then in the new boxes or stalls, a horse may roll, after a long and tiring journey, and if it rolls over against the wall or partition of the box, its legs may get wedged so that it cannot get up. If a horse panics in this position, it is sure to hurt itself unless someone, in whom it has complete confidence, arrives to calm and help it. Apart from these serious aspects of possible accident are the more psychological problems when a horse loses interest in its feed due to excitement and mental strain. A horse must eat to have the physical strength for long and tiring shows and therefore a variety of tit-bits in the meals have to be put in to maintain the horse's interest. A good groom takes as much time and trouble with his charges as a mother would take with her children.

A horse that is happy in the stable and has confidence in the groom is a much more relaxed and easier subject for the rider to work with. People who do not feel well cannot give a top-class performance when physical strain is involved, and horses are the same. They depend on the person who is looking after them to keep them happy, correctly fed, their injuries efficiently dressed and sometimes presupposed for treatment and to understand how each horse should be understood as a character. Paul had become an expert

[ 97 ]

in all these things after fourteen years' experience of travelling with my various horses.

Girls who approach me to find out if I have a place for them in the stables to undertake a similar life often do not understand how much this work entails. It requires great physical toughness to withstand long journeys in uncomfortable draughty trucks with horses, and trains that shunt in the night so violently that the horses fall unwittingly on top of the groom, when the engine hits the buffers with force. There is also needed the ability to put up with discomfort through a tour of international shows with poor sleeping and feeding facilities for the grooms and often poor stabling for the horses with which the rider hopes to win glory for the nation in big competitions. Out of competition hours a girl groom may find there are only men who look after the other team horses, and who do not speak a word of her language. It can be a lonely and hard life and yet the horses depend so much on the person who cares for them. That is where Paul's genius lies, in her ability to understand each horse and why it needs special attention, over and above the energy to cope with all the tough journeys, the unnecessary delays at frontiers, agents who have not provided the right papers, and the thousand other problems that can be encountered on a journey with horses.

At the White City it was Scorchin who pulled off the big competition of the John Player Trophy, up till then the biggest prize that had ever been given at the R.I.H.S. Flanagan missed the White City Stadium Cup, the 'choose your points' competition, by one end of a pole coming off the cup and resting on the hedge.

Flanagan came back to the country near his home where he first began work. At Durham he won the big championship after already dividing another at Blackpool. Dublin, Brighton, Ostend, St Gall followed and then we found ourselves at Hickstead for the Derby. A show jumper works hard for his living.

One fence down in the Derby put Flanagan equal second that year to the only clear round of Seamus Hayes on Goodbye. Poor Flanagan went lame on the first night of Wembley and so he did not jump again until the following April.

# CHAPTER 10

# The Wonderful Year

PAUL had been asking me for a long time, when I was going to buy another saddle, because we needed one desperately. I evaded the issue for some time because I secretly hoped that Flanagan might win a saddle one day. Also I had the financial responsibility in front of me of buying a house and land; I could hardly justify spending £40–£50 on a saddle when the other was of so much greater importance.

Flanagan, bless his heart, came once more to the rescue. He won me not one, but two saddles. The first he obtained at Hickstead in April 1962 for his consistent performance throughout the three days. The second was the saddle of honour won by the horse gaining the highest total marks during the White City Jumping Events. Before his achievement in London, he had two C.H.I.O.s abroad at Lucerne and Barcelona. These shows gave him four wins to his credit, and Great Britain won both the Nations Cups, although I rode Scorchin for this team event. The two horses also won me the Carven prize at each show.

A month later we were back at Hickstead, faced with the Derby course. The day before the Derby, a race meeting had been put on at Lingfield Park in aid of the Olympic Equestrian Fund. I was asked especially to attend, and so I cancelled my entries at Hickstead for that day. The weather was unkind which cut the crowd, but a good profit

General Franco watched us win our third European Ladies Championship held in
Madrid 1962

Flanagan and Scorchin having a winter's holiday in front of Sudgrove House

Flanagan in front of Miserden House

was still gained for the fund, because the Queen and Prince Philip came to the meeting. They created an atmosphere as cheerful as the weather was dull. The highlight of the racing came in the big race, when six horses were involved in a photo finish. After waiting for the official verdict of the camera, great was the delight when it was announced that the Queen's Aubusson was the winner.

The Derby had a little better weather and my horses were very fresh from their day's holiday. The older horses are always better when they are fit and fresh, which was strikingly proved last year when I kept Flanagan for only a few of the biggest competitions, which he came out and won. A young horse needs more regular work to gain confidence by the constant repetition of jumping over different courses.

Sinjon, ridden by the American team captain, was the favourite for the Derby as their team were training at Hickstead prior to the White City. Sinjon had already won on the first two days, including the Derby Trial event, at Hickstead. Before Bill Steinkraus jumped this good horse over the Derby fences, it was my turn on Scorchin. My grand trooper really enjoyed himself as he leapt around the course. The year before, he had fallen at an oxer but this year we jumped it safely. The bank he jumped for the first time, coming off it well and taking two strides to jump the post and rails beyond the 10' 6" drop. We continued clear and at the last fence which we met well, I thought we were over, but one of the rustic bars of the parallels fell after we landed to give us 4 faults. He must have dropped a hind hoof on it. It is no use searching for sympathy in these circumstances; in order to win one must try again on another horse or another year.

Into the ring came Sinjon who went clear as expected, as far as the bank. He suddenly took fright when he saw the big drop, stopped and reined back a couple of steps before being kicked forward to jump down safely. The rest of his round was clear but he had three faults for the technical disobedience at the bank which put him ahead of the horses with 4 faults and the best so far.

Thirty-seven of the fifty-four horses entered in the Derby had already jumped before Tommy Wade came in on his fantastically brave and clever little Dundrum. This small bay horse is by a thoroughbred stallion 'Little Heaven' out of a Connemara pony. Although he had broken a blood vessel during the competition on the day before and had to be led out of the ring with a bad nose-bleed, he came in for the Derby with his ears pricked. Without the semblance of a mistake he made light work of a clear round over the sixteen fences. Only 3 minutes is allowed to jump this course of twenty-four actual jumping efforts in a distance of 1,305 yards.

In the first Derby of 1961, only one horse was clear, the Irish 'Goodbye', ridden by Seamus Hayes, out of forty-eight starters. People thought that again the prize would go unchallenged to Ireland. Flanagan decided otherwise and, making up for his one fence down the year before, he did all that I asked of him. I took just as much care with Flanagan as I had with Scorchin, coming into the last fence, but *he* picked up his hind heels, well clear of the rustic rails.

Down the bank we had taken off in exactly the same place as with Scorchin, so as to jump well out and be in the right stride before the post and rails at 4' 7". The bank had caused trouble to Anneli Drummond-Hay, whose Merely-a-Monarch slid down the face, which put him wrong for the rails only thirty-three feet away. A horse needed to jump off the face of the bank in order to keep balanced. Harvey Smith was lucky to get away clear over the fence after the bank in spite of taking four strides on Farmer's Boy, but this horse is an exception and known to be able to put in twice as many strides in half the distance as any other horse. Sudden nearly put Mary Barnes on the floor when he leapt straight from the top of the bank. He hit the ground with his nose, too, and then Mary could not balance him for the rails, which he had down. The only mistake that Oorskiet made with Lady Sarah Fitzalan Howard was to take off much too far from the water, so that he landed well in it for 4 faults. Five other horses had one fault over the course, but at different fences. No jump penalized the horses more than any other, which is the proof of a well-built course.

The grey skies had turned into drizzle by the time of the jump-off. Dundrum was first to go. He was jumping brilliantly when I was astonished to see the white and fairly solid barrier, that followed the open water, fall. I had been working out how I could beat him on time, but not on faults. Flanagan's problem was to jump the water clear and, with this in mind, I started more quickly than Dundrum. I took the oxer with a wide turn to give Flanagan all the impulsion that he needed as the fence had been raised. As we came into the water on a galloping stride, my heart dropped when I saw that we were not accurate enough for an exact take-off. Flanagan would not help me out here so a quick check and restriding of three galloping paces got us to the pole of the take-off and over the tape on the landing side—clear.

After this we steadied a little and Flanagan finished clear

over the last fences. He had won the Derby—and I began to realize that the unexpected had happened. Flanagan entered the arena again—doing his parade walk—and he knew the importance of his achievement. When the garland of oak leaves was placed around his neck to acknowledge his win, a glint came into his eyes. We have to keep him short of hay in order to preserve his figure for jumping. He saw an unprecedented opportunity and quickly grabbed a mouthful of oak leaves. Douggie Bunn, the organizer of Hickstead, patiently tied the broken ribbon again around his neck. Flan had another go at the leaves while I was receiving the golden trophy of a horse. This time he hung on and severed the central wire!

Eventually we cantered around with the oak leaves draped about, rather than encircling, his neck. I had my work cut out to secure the garland and clutch the medal that he won for being the best horse that had completed Badminton or the Grand National course; and also I held the tankard won by Scorchin for the best owner-ridden horse. He had been the fastest four faults to win the trophy given by Colonel Mike Ansell.

As though this excitement were not enough, there was yet more in store. First the horses had over a week to rest and then we started once again at the White City. To begin with, things just did not click, with Flanagan beaten by inside a second in the final jump-off for the Horse and Hound Cup. Both my horses had one fence down in the Queen's Cup to put them equal third, only two clear rounds being jumped. Judy Crago jumped another clear round to win.

In the Nations Cup I rode Scorchin, but the rain unkindly made the ground into a veritable quagmire. Unfortunately, he slipped at a double and gave me a fall in the first round. Although we were clear, apart from this misfortune, I felt very muzzy as I had hit the back of my head hard, in spite of the superficial mud of the arena. Scorchin carried me clear over the worst fences in the last line, after I had remounted. I did not jump the second round, as our team was out of the running; thus the effort, when neither of us was quite fit, would have been of no help.

The next night, in the John Player Trophy, I again rode Scorchin who had won this prize the year before. It was a pity that he ran out in a treble, but he was excused because of the fright from his fall the day before, although we were otherwise clear. O'Malley, a Canadian horse bought by Bob Hanson the previous winter and ridden by Harvey Smith, won the competition. Posillipo, the danger to Scorchin, during the last year's thrilling finish, was beaten into second place. Flanagan made up for Scorchin's misdemeanour by winning the White City Stadium Cup with 880 points in both rounds, out of the mud. This clinched his saddle of honour for the best horse throughout the show.

Less than a year later I heard that the Worshipful Company of Saddlers was to honour me by the bestowal of membership in their ancient Company, following the revival by the Court of a nomenclature which had fallen into disuse. This enables them to honour ladies and gentlemen who may be considered to have rendered outstanding services to equitation in this country. The Court invited me to become one of the new 'Yeomen'. Consequently at the Saddlers' Hall, in Gutter Lane, Cheapside, I took the oath for admission as a Yeoman of the Worshipful Company of Saddlers—a most notable and memorable occasion for me.

On Saturday the White City arena was holding more than on any other day and the horses were really sucking their feet out of the mud. It was lucky that although I knew that Flanagan could not operate in this going, it did not deter Scorchin. After he had jumped two clear rounds, we came to the final jump-off. Joy of joys, no one else was clear, but Scorchin again pulled up his undercarriage over each fence and finished with the only faultless round. This was his second victory as Champion of Champions in the *Daily Mail* Cup. He now had emulated Prince Hal's achievement. At that moment I was more than surprised and happy that Scorchin had given me my fourth Gold Cup. The *Daily Mail* Gold Cup for the Championship of the White City is the only one that a rider can win outright. The other cups are perpetual challenge cups that have to be returned each year. This year his win also gave me the Loriners Cup for the best result with two horses throughout the show. Not only was I delighted to win this lovely trophy, but as I had recently become an honorary member of the Worshipful Company of Loriners, I could now feel that I had partly justified their Court's decision to make me a member of their Guild.

So my horses' clothing is almost covered by the three Guilds of which I am an honorary member. There is the Saddlers for the saddlery, the Loriners for the bits and spurs, and the Farriers for the shoes. My frequent contributions by purchasing these products must have already ensured the future prosperity of the trades!

It has always been a rush to get home from the White City and then to set straight off for Blackpool. The National Championships have until this year been held there at the Royal Lancs Show and so if one wanted to defend a title, the relentless tour had to be continued. During the day and two nights spent at home between the week in London and the tour of the North, our washing machine could be heard constantly humming. Dozens of shirts, trousers, breeches, horse sheets, stocks and ties, all had to be washed, dried and ironed before setting off again. The back of the car, when it returns from one of these long show tours, looks as though it holds the complete stock for a rummage sale. The girls have a worse time because they have to unpack the horses' luggage too. The horsebox is turned into living quarters at the shows, and so they have to stock up with food, Calor gas, crockery, camp-beds, blankets and changes of clothes. If the show is a wet one, everything gets muddy. I think that our home quick clean and dry service, together with restocking, re-equipping and refuelling, has been developed to a finer art than could ever be boasted by any publicized professional company.

The White City week had been wet, but the lorry when it left for Blackpool was fully stocked with clean and dry clothing for horses and girls alike. Flanagan justified the journey by winning the Ladies National Championship at Blackpool and then the big open class at Kingston-on-Soar. Unfortunately he slipped as he cantered round with his rosette and hit a nerve below his hock, with his other hoof, from which he did not recover until Wembley in October. My chief fun at this show came from swimming in an indoor pool, built by Lord Belper in a disused wing of the house. The water was heated, and so one could glance through the misted windows at the rain falling outside, whilst one turned somersaults on the trapeze, swam, dived and eventually emerged rather pink from the warmth of the water. Riders do not often have the luxury of these facilities!

Flanagan was out of action for nearly two months and so I busied myself by going abroad, but first I got myself knocked out by a kick on the head at a local show. The black eye only took about ten days to go on that occasion.

Autumn mists and Wembley at the beginning of October came almost at Michaelmas, the same time as the take-over date of my new home at Sudgrove and the start of converting garages back to stables for the horses. My mind was probably concentrating rather more on Sudgrove than on the Horse of the Year Show. It was Flanagan who brought me back to the job in hand. He had been second the year before in the Leading Show Jumper Competition and now he was determined to better this result. I had won the first Leading Show Jumper competition with Finality at Harringay in 1949, thirteen years before, and then again on Mr Pollard in 1958 at the last Harringay Show. Now at Wembley we had a wide treble for the penultimate fence, a difficult fence for Flanagan to reach. The higher the fences became, the more he had to reach for them. However, we were both trying very hard.

After three rounds over a gradually heightened course, only Franco, Royal Lord and Flanagan were still clear. The wall which came as the last part of the treble had the bar beyond it raised and widened, which was Flanagan's chief worry. The other fences were put up too. Franco and Royal Lord both jumped before me, and both hit the big parallel poles which came as the third fence. Royal Lord had been fast, but we worked now for a clear round. Riding right into the corner of the small arena I gave Flanagan the maximum impetus to jump the big treble, as he had already cleared the bogey fence that had caught the other two horses. Kicking him and encouraging him every stride to the treble, and keeping him going even in mid-air so that he would get close enough to the last wall of the treble, took all my powers. Over the wall, he felt that he still could not get the spread and so he threw up his head in order to make an extra effort. He pulled the necessary inch out of the bag and only touched the far pole on top, so that it did not fall. I had been pushing him to make him reach the spread and when he threw up his head he dislocated my thumb on his neck.

My thumb was loose, but I checked him severely for the turn to the last upright fence and we jumped it clear—winner of the Leading Show Jumper of the Year 1962.

We were interviewed on television after the presentation and Flanagan was an awful fool. I was afraid that he would wreck either himself or the cameras, or even Dorian Williams who was interviewing us. I am not sure which of us was the more excited.

We were delighted to get a day or two at home, before we set out once more. Our destination was Spain, for the European Ladies Championship to be held in Madrid. Flanagan and Scorchin were travelling with Paul by air, together with Judy Crago's two horses, Thou Swell and Spring Fever, her partner when winning the Queen's Cup in July. The chartered plane had also to pick up some Dutch horses in Amsterdam. After these extra horses had been put aboard, the plane was very loath to leave the ground. In Bordeaux the pilot had to make an extra landing to ensure that he had enough fuel to climb over the Pyrenees. The runway there was barely long enough for the loaded take-off but the aircraft became airborne just in time.

This anxious trip in the plane was not the end of the nerve strain for Pauline. The loading of the horses at

Amsterdam and the extra refuelling at Bordeaux had taken so long that it was past midnight when the plane landed at Barajas, the Madrid airport. A lorry had been sent to meet the horses, but it only had a narrow and steep plank as a ramp, for the horses to clamber up and into the truck.

Flanagan was taken out of the plane by one of the personnel waiting there, while Paul stayed with Scorchin ready to follow out of the plane. As she came down the plane ramp with Scorchin, she was horrified to see, through the darkness, the man who had Flanagan walk up the lorry plank and stop at the top. Flanagan who was bustling up behind him, had to stop suddenly too, and to get his balance on the steep slope of the plank, he put a hind leg back, but off the plank. He fell backwards off the ramp and was very lucky not to break a leg. When he got to his feet, he had a very sore hock and was sorry for himself.

The next morning I went to the stables by the lovely show ground in the Club, and Paul told me of the near disaster. After seeing him trot and then riding him for a time, I decided not to jump Flanagan in the first competition. The ladies championship classes did not start until the next day.

Scorchin enjoyed himself galloping over the first course, against the clock, and was placed with his clear round. The next day we had the same type of competition. The course for the first leg of the ladies championship proved to be quite difficult and there was only one clear round. The win went to Spain's only lady representative, Paula Elizalde de Goyoaga, riding her husband Paco's brilliant little French-bred chestnut. The crowd was naturally delighted.

Flanagan had jumped the fastest round, but just tipped off a rustic rail into a pen, where we had to jump into and then

turn out through a gap on the left. Judy Crago had one
refusal, but her time was faster than Mrs Helga Köhler of
Germany, who also had a stop. This put Judy and me in
second and fourth places.

Used as we are to getting wet at shows in England,
Madrid gave us the full treatment. However, the rain
eased a little for the Puissance competition the next day.
Judy and I were clear on both our horses in the first round,
and Paula was clear on Kif-Kif. In the only jump-off both
Judy and I were again clear on the first horses we rode,
Thou Swell and Flanagan, and so did not have to ride our
second horses as they would not have counted. Paula was
also clear again and so the three of us divided the first prize.

Before our final contest the ground had become sodden
with heavy rain. The committee decided to cancel the
other events leaving only our final. The start was put back
to 5 p.m. as Generalissimo Franco and his wife were coming
to watch. The show ground bristled with armed police
for this honour.

A big course was fairly set, with the second fence a
double of a spread in and straight gates out. The third
fence was a straight wall in and a spread fence out.

Before the water, which had a small brush on the take-off
side, there was a big wall, and following the water a turn
led left to straight rails. Another double of straight rustic
poles jumped in two short strides was placed towards the
exit, where the horses were onward bound.

The first horse in was a representative for Italy called
Cecil, who collected a cricket score with refusals. This
gave me no line that the set time was very short. Flanagan,
next to go, rolled off the pole of the spread into the second
fence, a double, but jumping well, he was clear over the

[ 111 ]

rest. Although he had gone a good gallop he had half a time fault.

The others then realized that the time was very short and cut all the corners to compensate. Nico jumped the first clear, with Anna Clement going a terrific gallop, but the horse was very tired when he finished. Judy Crago then raised our hopes with a lovely clear on Spring Fever. Kif-Kif collected 8 faults, but Helga Köhler on Cremona went clear.

Cecil had been withdrawn, and so Flanagan was first into the ring for the second round. By then the going had deteriorated and was very deep in places, but this time he went clear although he got bogged down once or twice. Nico had 8 faults on this round, having the last two fences down.

The stage was set for Spring Fever who was in the best position for points. All went well until the ninth fence, the rustic double, where she ran out. After this nothing went right and by the end of the course there was a disastrous score of twenty-eight faults. Ominously the mare's name had been misprinted in the programme as 'Spring Fewer'.

Giulia Serventi and Doli finished with a total of 9¾ faults, and Paula de Goyoaga did not go well on Kif-Kif in the second round and they finished with 19½ faults, which displaced them from the top of the list.

Four faults for Helga Köhler on Cremona brought her up to second place, with Flanagan winning the championship for the third time. Paula was third with Kif-Kif. The Generalissimo presented his cup, and the parade was led by the mounted guard.

It was a proud moment for me to receive the cup. General Franco laughed when I reminded him of the

occasion in 1954 when he had been about to present me
with the cup for the Grand Prix—but, alas, I had been
overcome by the Madrid bug at the great moment and so
was *non compos mentis*, having passed out in a faint!

My faithful Flanagan had done his part in getting our
third gold Ladies European Championship medal. For the
second year running Great Britain held the Men's, Ladies
and Junior European Championship. I hope that he may
be able to enjoy helping us to win on many more occasions
in the future. His jumping career in the top flight has
already lasted longer than most horses. Still he would be
disappointed if he thought there were not many more
rosettes to adorn his ears, parades where he could point his
toes proudly while doing his parade walk and, of course,
some juicy garlands around his neck for a handy snack while
he receives his prize—and he deserves every mouthful.

I was sad to leave Flanagan as though he had jumped
his last clear round. Just as Mark Twain read his obituary
in the local press and told the editor that it was a little
premature, so Flanagan has just proved that our partnership is not yet moribund. At Hickstead in July we won
the European Ladies Championship for the third time
running and the fourth time in all. Flanagan has helped
me on all these occasions, with Prince Hal in the first year
of this competition in 1957 and since then with Scorchin.
This year it was his effort alone that won the points for
the three legs of the Championship.

He was slightly disappointed that he was not allowed
to jump in the Hickstead Derby that he had won the
year before, when he had profited by eating his victor's
laurels. This time he had only a ribbon tied round his
neck, which did not stimulate his appetite. Perhaps I felt

the emotion of the moment more deeply than Flanagan, because I had not expected him to beat better and younger horses. More important to me was the joy that this was the last Championship that I would compete in under my own name. Bob Hanson was not able to be present for the Championship but his faith in our partnership had been fully justified.

Now both Flanagan and I will go ahead to do as well as we can at our own chosen moments. His chosen moment is now. He demands immediate attention with a large carrot, so please excuse me as I must go and give him this small reward.